European Coordination Centre for Research
and Documentation in Social Sciences

URBAN EUROPE: A Study of Growth
and Decline

Volume 1

The Costs of Urban Growth (CURB) Project

This major research project from the *European Coordination Centre for Research and Documentation in Social Sciences* (the Vienna Centre) will be published under the general title of URBAN EUROPE. The following titles make up the series.

VAN DEN BERG, L. *et al.*
Urban Europe: A Study of Growth and Decline (Volume 1)
MONTANARI, A. (Ed.)
Urban Europe: Development Trends and Urban Policies: National Experiences (Volume 2)
DREWETT, R. & ROSSI, A.
Urban Europe: Settlement Structure and Change 1950–1980 (Volume 3)
REGULSKI, J. (Ed.)
Urban Europe: Urban Change and Urban Policies: A Cross-national Annotated Bibliography (Volume 4)
SCHUBERT, U. (Ed.)
Urban Europe: Towards a Theory of Urban Systems' Change (Volume 5)
HÖRCHER, N. & MATTHIESSEN, C. (Eds.)
Urban Europe: Medium-sized Towns in Transition: A Case Study Perspective (Volume 6)
MAGNUSSEN, J., REGULSKI, J. & SENN, L. (Eds.)
Urban Europe: Urban Policy Analysis and Evaluation (Volume 7)
DZIEMBOWSKI, Z. & LACOUR, C. (Eds.)
Urban Europe: Costs of Urban Growth (Volume 8)
MUSIC, B. & DREWETT, R.
Urban Europe: National Settlement Strategies and Policy Responses (Volume 9)

Other Publications of the Vienna Centre

AMANN, A.
Open Care for the Elderly in Seven European Countries
BERTING, J., MILLS, S. C. & WINTERSBERGER, H.
The Socio-economic Impact of Microelectronics
CAO-PINNA, V. & SHATALIN, S.
Consumption Patterns in Eastern and Western Europe
DURAND-DROUHIN, J.-L. & SZWENGRUB, L.-M.
Rural Community Studies in Europe, Volumes 1 & 2
FORSLIN, J., SARAPATA, A. & WHITEHILL, A.
Automation and Industrial Workers, Volume 1, Parts 1 & 2 and Volume 2
MIHAILESCU, I. & MENDRAS, H.
Theory and Methodology in Rural Community Studies
PENOUIL, M. & PETRELLA, R.
The Location of Growing Industries in Europe
SZALAI, A. & PETRELLA, R.
Cross-national Comparative Survey Research: Theory and Practice

NOTICE TO READERS

Dear Reader,

If your library is not already a standing/continuation order customer to the above series, may we recommend that you place a standing/continuation order to receive all new volumes immediately upon publication. Should you find that these volumes no longer serve your needs, your order may be cancelled at any time without notice.

ROBERT MAXWELL
Publisher at Pergamon Press

URBAN EUROPE A Study of Growth and Decline

by

Leo van den Berg
Roy Drewett
Leo H. Klaassen
Angelo Rossi
Cornelis H. T. Vijverberg

*for the European Coordination Centre
for Research and Documentation in
Social Sciences*

Volume 1 of Urban Europe

PERGAMON PRESS

Oxford · New York · Toronto
Sydney · Paris · Frankfurt

U.K.	Pergamon Press Ltd., Headington Hill Hall, Oxford OX3 0BW, England
U.S.A.	Pergamon Press Inc., Maxwell House, Fairview Park, Elmsford, New York 10523, U.S.A.
CANADA	Pergamon Press Canada Ltd., Suite 104, 150 Consumers Road, Willowdale, Ontario M2J IP9, Canada
AUSTRALIA	Pergamon Press (Aust.) Pty. Ltd., P.O. Box 544, Potts Point, N.S.W. 2011, Australia
FRANCE	Pergamon Press SARL, 24 rue des Ecoles, 75240 Paris, Cedex 05, France
FEDERAL REPUBLIC OF GERMANY	Pergamon Press GmbH, 6242 Kronberg-Taunus, Hammerweg 6, Federal Republic of Germany

First edition 1982

British Library Cataloguing in Publication Data
Urban Europe
Vol. 1: A study of growth and decline.—(Cross national comparative series)
1. Cities and towns—Europe—Growth—History
I. Berg, Leo van den
II. European Coordination Centre for Research and Documentation in Social Sciences
III. Series
306.7'6'094   HT131

ISBN 0-08-023156-X
Library of Congress Catalog Card No.: 81-81233

Printed in Great Britain by A. Wheaton & Co. Ltd., Exeter

Preface

The *Urban Europe* series presents the results of a cross-national comparative study into the Costs of Urban Growth. The study, known by the acronym CURB, was undertaken on behalf of the European Coordination Centre for Research and Documentation in Social Sciences (the Vienna Centre) by research teams from 14 countries in Eastern and Western Europe.

The general aim of the CURB project, as the name implies, has been to study the financing of urban systems and to evaluate the costs associated with urban change. The relevance of such a policy-oriented project seemed self-evident at the start and seems even more so now, with the prospect of European cities being transformed by radically changing locational preferences, and with the spectre of city and national governments grappling to devise policies that meet the varied needs of growing and declining urban areas alike. As many of the countries participating in the CURB project have different administrative systems, varied levels of economic development and urbanization, and contrasting cultural norms, a wide range of urban policy experiences can be compared with regard to their impact and effectiveness.

Although the aim was clear, albeit a daunting one, the choice of concepts, methods, and level of analysis was not. This required lengthy and careful evaluation with a modicum of "learning by doing" given the paucity of experience in the field of comparative urban studies. Following a feasibility study into urban change and urban expenditures, it was decided to examine the cost question in the context of the urban development process and to conduct the analysis at the ecological and case-study levels. The project was organized in two main stages.

In *Stage 1*, the whole group worked on common lines, viz. to elaborate a conceptual framework of urban systems' change; to establish a macrolevel data-base for municipalities of over 10,000 population and for Functional Urban Regions (FURs) of over 200,000; to prepare country reports on urban change and national settlement strategies; and to complete a

v

selected annotated bibliography of related urban research. Problems of data comparability were overcome as far as it was feasible by having common guidelines for data collection. The overall work programme was discussed and agreed upon at the project's six-monthly General Meetings. The comparative research was undertaken by a small team which met more frequently. This stage of the study was coordinated by the project's Steering Committee and Scientific Secretary, the latter working full-time in Vienna.

In *Stage 2* the project has had a more decentralized structure. There has been one common task—namely, the preparation of a detailed case-study of a medium-sized FUR in each country, again following common guidelines. Meanwhile, four Working Groups have prepared: an elaboration of the theory of urban systems' change; a comparative analysis of the case-study data-base; and a formulation of relevant methodologies for urban policy and urban cose evaluation. Although more emphasis has been given to sessions of the different working groups, the continuity required in the project has been maintained through regular General Meetings, and the study has been coordinated by the project's Executive Committee and the Scientific Secretary.

Each of the various components of the two stages are published in the *Urban Europe* series under the titles listed in the front of this volume. The names of all the CURB project participants, members of the Steering Committee for Stage 1, the Executive Committee for Stage 2, the Chairmen of Working Groups, and the Scientific Secretaries of the project are listed below.

We would like to place on record our gratitude for the help and encouragement the CURB project has received from many quarters. National teams were supported by their universities and institutes, academies of sciences, foundations, research councils, banks, and other funding institutions. A full acknowledgement of this support will be forthcoming in the volumes containing national contributions. In the meantime, we express our gratitude for this support: without it the project would not have existed. We are indebted for the long-standing support given to us by the Board of Directors and staff of the Vienna Centre. In particular, to Professor Adam Schaff, Riccardo Petrella, and Stephen Mills. Their commitment and enthusiasm for comparative research was a great source of stimulation. We also appreciate highly the friendly help we receive from the permanent members of the Centre's staff, especially Simone Porges, Elizabeth Altschul, and Gunilla Vyskovsky. And not least, our Scientific Secretaries, the linchpin of the project, often left to plough a lonely furrow on our behalf in the inner sanctums of Grünangergasse. We owe a great debt to all of them for their valiant efforts. Lastly, there is the contribution made by Pergamon Press in Oxford who have done much more than be the publisher of the *Urban Europe* series. Robert Maxwell and Peggy Ducker have always received us with great courtesy and been unstinting in their cooperation. The publishers'·generous backing of some editorial meetings has made a crucial difference. We are indebted to them for this help.

Finally, we would like to record with considerable pleasure the contribution made to the project by Professor Gaston Gaudard and Professor Jean Valarche, University of Fribourg, Switzerland. It was their original initiative that convinced the Vienna Centre to set up the study, and their early efforts that succeeded in launching it.

1. *Participants and Institutions (in alphabetical order)*

Austria
Gerhard CLEMENZ, Peter FINDL, Richard GISSER, Marcus METELKA and Uwe SCHUBERT
—Austrian Central Statistical Office, Vienna.
—University of Vienna, Institute for Quantitative Economic Theory.
—Vienna Economic University, Institute of Urban and Regional Studies.

Belgium
Hugo ABTS, Herman BAEYENS and Bonnie WALTER
—Mens en Ruimte, vzw. Brussels.

Bulgaria
Hristo GANEV, Gesho GESHEV and Peter POPOV
—Bulgarian Academy of Sciences, Institute of Geography, Sofia.
—University of Sofia, Faculty of Geology and Geography.

Denmark
Jan MAGNUSEN and Christian MATTHIESSEN
—University of Copenhagen, Institute of Geography.

France
Maurice GOZE and Claude LACOUR
—University of Bordeaux, South West Regional Economic Institute.

Germany, Federal Republic of
Hartmut DANNEBERG
—BBE—Consulting Nordheim Düsseldorf.

Great Britain
Bob ARMSTRONG, Roy DREWETT, Mike HARLEY, Margaret HOBSON and Margaret JEFFERY
—University of Birmingham, Water Industry Management Unit.
—University of London, The London School of Economics and Political Sciences.

Hungary
Eta DAROCZI, Nora HÖRCHER, Ester HORVATH and Gyorgy VUKOVICH
—Hungarian Academy of Sciences, Geographical Research Institute, Budapest.
—Hungarian Central Statistical Office, Budapest.
—Hungarian Institute for Town and Regional Planning (VATI), Budapest.

Italy
Angel CALOIA and Lanfranco SENN
—Catholic University of Milan, Department of Economics.
—Centre for Social Analysis (CLAS), Milan.
—University of Trento, Department of Economics.

Netherlands
Leo van den BERG, Sjaak BOECKHOUT, Leo H. KLAASSEN, Jan van der MEER and Kees VIJVERBERG
—Erasmus University of Rotterdam, Economic Faculty, Department for Spatial Economics.
—Netherlands Economic Institute, Rotterdam.
—Netherlands Organization for the Advancement of Pure Research (ZWO), The Hague.

Poland
Zygmund DZIEMBOWSKI, Stanislav HERMAN and Jerzy REGULSKI
—Main School of Planning and Statistics of Warsaw, Institute of Urban Economy and Housing Policy.
—Polish Academy of Sciences, Committee for Space Economy and Regional Planning, Warsaw.
—University of Łódź, Institute of Regional Policies.

Sweden
Lars ELSTRÖM, Einar HOLM and Lars SANDSTRÖM
—University of Umeå, Department of Geography.

Switzerland
Janos DOZSA, Angelo ROSSI and Pier Angelo TAMI
—Swiss Federal High School of Technology of Zürich, Institute for National, Regional and Local Planning.

Yugoslavia
Metka BLEJEC, Lojze GOSAR and Vladimir B. MUSIC
—Urban Planning Institute of S.R. Slovenia, Ljubljana.

2. Coordinators of the Project

Co-Directors for the Feasibility Stage (1973–1974)

Gaston GAUDARD	Switzerland
Roy DREWETT	Great Britain

Steering Committee for Stage 1 (1975–1978)

Roy DREWETT (*Chairman*)	Great Britain
Angelo CALOIA	Italy
Zygmund DZIEMBOWSKI	Poland
Leo KLAASSEN	Netherlands
Claude LACOUR	France
Braco MUSIC	Yugoslavia
Gyorgy VUKOVICH	Hungary

Steering Committee for Stage 2 1979–1982)

Roy DREWETT (*Chairman*)	Great Britain
Angelo CALOIA	Italy
Zygmund DZIEMBOWSKI	Poland
Nora HÖRCHER	Hungary
Uwe SCHUBERT	Austria
Lanfranco SENN	Italy

Chairmen of Working Groups (1977–1982)

Urban Systems Group	Uwe SCHUBERT	Austria
Urban Policy Group	Lanfranco SENN	Italy
Data Analysis Group	Nora HÖRCHER and	Hungary
	Chris MATTHEISSEN	Denmark
Urban Costs Group	Zymund DZIEMBOWSKI and	Poland
	Claude LACOUR	France

Scientific Secretaries at the Vienna Centre

Riccardo PETRELLA	Italy	1971–1972
Eta DAROCZI	Hungary	1972–1975
Markus METELKA	Austria	1975–1978
Helmut WINTERSBERGER	Austria	1978–1979
Armando MONTANARI	Italy	1979–1982

Preface to Volume 1

The results presented here in Volume 1 are those produced as part of the first stage. It contains the initital conceptual framework which incorporates some elements of a behavioural theory of the spatial welfare-functions of key actors in the urban transformation process, viz. households, employers and governments. This is linked to the dynamics of human settlement systems conceived in "life-cycle" terms. A cross-national comparative analysis of urban change for the sample of municipalities and FURs (Functional Urban Regions), and a classification of actual urban policies and policy instruments, are then related to the behavioural and structural postulates.

It should be stressed that the data-base used in the preparation of this book, a set of relevant and comparable figures for a large number of urban municipalities and FURs, could never have been established without the intensive help and cooperation of all the CURB participants. They also contributed considerably to the theoretical part of the study by discussing draft documents, suggesting improvements and drafting amendments. Their collective commitment to the project and the *esprit de corps* they engendered was the basic reason why the team overcame many obstacles. They all deserve our thanks for their contribution to an East–West project which is of considerable importance to the societal development and policy in each of the countries.

In addition, we thank all those who helped with other tasks associated with the preparation of this volume. In particular, to Margaret Jeffery (London School of Economics) and Janos Dozsa (Eidgenossische Technische Hochschule, Zürich) who assisted with the computer programming of the urban change analysis; to Mrs. A. C. A. Elderson (Netherlands Economic Institute, Rotterdam) for the editing and translation work of the first draft of the manuscript; to Polly Buston who undertook the task of linguistic editing with skill and imagination; and to Jeanne Marie Stanton for the meticulous preparation of the artwork.

Volume 1 was written by Leo van den Berg (Erasmus University, Rotterdam), Roy Drewett (London School of Economics), Leo H. Klaassen (Netherlands Economic Institute, Rotterdam), Angelo Rossi (Eidgenossische Technische Hochschule, Zürich), and Kees Vijverberg (Netherlands Economic Institute, Rotterdam), with quotes from *Elements of a Theory of Urbanization Processes in Socialist Countries* by Stanislav Herman and Jerzy Regulski (CURB Project Working Document 3/77).

Contents

INTRODUCTION   xv

Part I. ELEMENTS OF A THEORY OF URBAN DEVELOPMENT

1. INTRODUCTION   3

2. THE ACTORS IN THE URBAN SYSTEM   8

2.1. *Households as actors in the urban system*   8
2.2. *The industrial sector as an actor in the urban system*   15
   2.2.1. *Objectives and locational behaviour*   16
   2.2.2. *Demand and supply potentials*   17
   2.2.3. *The dynamics of industrial behaviour*   19
2.3. *The government as an actor in the urban system*   20

3. STAGES OF URBAN DEVELOPMENT   24

3.1. *The first stage: urbanization*   25
3.2. *The second stage: suburbanization*   29
3.3. *The third stage: desurbanization and inter-urban decentralization*   34
   3.3.1. *The national settlement system*   40
3.4. *The future: reurbanization?*   40
   3.4.1. *Stages of desurbanization*   40
   3.4.2. *The consequences of desurbanization*   43

Part II. EMPIRICAL ANALYSIS OF URBAN DEVELOPMENT TRENDS

4. INTRODUCTION   49

4.1. *Objectives*   49
4.2. *Concepts, methods, and definitions*   49
   4.2.1. *Problems in cross-national comparative research*   50
   4.2.2. *Samples of urban municipalities*   53

5. THE SAMPLE OF FUNCTIONAL URBAN REGIONS   55

6. TRENDS OF URBAN DEVELOPMENT: URBAN MUNICIPALITIES, 1960–1970   61

6.1. *Population change by size group*   61
6.2. *The regional distribution of urban change*   64
6.3. *Urban change and the functional classification of urban municipalities and regions*   67

xiv

6.4. The demographic components of urban change 69
6.5. The relation between employment and population change 74
6.6. Some conclusions 75

7. TRENDS IN URBAN DEVELOPMENT: FUNCTIONAL URBAN REGIONS, 1950–1975 77

7.1. Population-growth performance by urban zones 77
7.2. Stages of urban development: a classification of FUR 81
7.3. Variation in FUR development trends, 1960–1970 83
7.4. Urban-development stages, 1950–1975 85
7.5. Urban trends in each dominant stage of development 92
7.6. Summary 101

Part III. ELEMENTS OF A THEORY ON URBAN POLICY AND AN EVALUATION OF NATIONAL URBAN POLICIES IN EUROPE

8. INTRODUCTION 105

9. A THEORY OF URBAN POLICY 106

9.1. What is urban policy? 106
9.2. Components of urban policy 112
9.3. Motives for urban policy 118

10. INTRODUCTION TO THE EVALUATION OF NATIONAL URBAN POLICIES IN EUROPE 121

11. URBAN POLICY IN RELATION TO CORE REGIONS 124

11.1. Introduction 124
11.2. Urban policy in the urbanization phase 125
11.3. Towards a national plan for urban development 128
11.4. Growth limitation and suburbanization 130
11.5. Town reconstruction and town renovation 138

12. URBAN POLICY IN PROBLEM AREAS 141

12.1. General remarks 141
12.2. Migration policy 142
12.3. Regional stimulation policy 144
    12.3.1. Motives and execution 144
    12.3.2. Regional policy as a form of explicit urban planning 146

13. THE NATURE OF PLANNING 149

MATHEMATICAL APPENDIX

1. GOVERNMENT EXPENDITURE, POTENTIALS AND WELFARE 155

1.1. Governmental welfare policy 155
1.2. Potentials and government expenditure 156

2. OPTIMUM ALLOCATION OF WELFARE INVESTMENTS 158

2.1. Approach for two facilities and n regions 158
2.2. The solution of the system 161

Introduction

In the most simple pattern underlying regional policy, a distinction is made between prosperous areas on the one hand and distressed areas on the other. Usually the criteria by which such a distinction is made are relatively simple ones. They relate either to the employment situation (e.g. unemployment rate) or to the level of GDP per head of the population or per head of the working population. Quite often the distressed areas are peripheral areas or areas with a one-sided economy in which the dominant sector is declining. Textile and coal-mining are well-known examples of sectors whose decline brought distress to many a European region. In many countries measures are taken to improve the situation. They range from financial assistance to new or expanding industries to the improvement of the social and technical infrastructure; all of them contribute directly or indirectly to the improvement of the economic and social structure of the depressed regions.

For such regions diversification is considered the most important objective. New and varied activities introduced to replace traditional ones spell not only new workplaces for the people but also economic stability for the region. For urbanized regions—often also the most prosperous ones—on the contrary, a policy of restraint is often advocated, the instruments being licence or permit systems, extra taxation on new investments, and restrictions on the creation of infrastructure, in particular technical infrastructure for private cars. It is felt that continued rapid urbanization of the regions around large agglomerations would in the long run boost economic costs to dizzy heights and plunge the environment into gloomy depths. Prospectives daunting enough to justify a policy of restraint.

It is easy to see why the governments of several countries believed that perhaps the problems of areas in distress as well as those of the large agglomerations could be solved by measures promoting the diversion of new activities, and even the relocation of existing ones, to underprivileged regions. Such measures, it was felt, could kill two birds with one stone: the agglomerations would be checked in their growth, while distressed areas would gain prosperity and stability.

Such policies were specifically pursued in the United Kingdom and the Netherlands, indirectly by trying to push entrepreneurs in the desired direction, directly by locating or relocating government institutions outside the large agglomerations. Owing to deliberate deconcentration, many government agencies in both countries are now established far from the madding crowd.

However, such policies express a way of thinking that is basically static; it assumes that a policy measure can transform an existing, stable but unfavourable situation into a new, equally stable but favourable, situation, and that is comparative statics at its purest!

A small shift in the assumption is enough to change the judgement of the present situation appreciably. For if we assume that regions on the one hand may have a better or worse income or employment situation than the national average, and on the other hand, may grow faster or slower than the national average, we arrive at four, instead of two, types of regions, while at the same time introducing the dynamic element into our considerations. If *per capita* income is taken to be the dominant factor, the four categories to be considered are the following.

First, the regions with income level and income growth both below the national average; they are the really depressed areas. Their present situation is bad and, unless their growth rate picks up, their future is even bleaker. Second, at the other end of the scale there are the regions that boast above-average income levels and growth rates. These are the prosperous areas. Third, the regions with below-average income levels but above-average growth rates (potentially prosperous areas), and fourth, areas where the income level exceeds the national average but the growth rate is below par (potentially depressed areas).

In the context of present developments it is the latter two categories, so far mostly not clearly distinguished in regional policy, that deserve special attention.

Once we have abandoned the all too simple belief that policy measures should just make for the transition from the present, undesirable situation to a better one, and have recognized—as we did at the beginning of this Introduction—the internal dynamics of regional development, we shall set out to learn about the basic factors that have governed regional developments through time and about the changes to be expected in the future. In other words, we need to know

(a) what factors have determined developments in the past, and
(b) what factors will determine developments in the future.

Under the conventional approach there are also two questions to be answered, viz.

(c) what factors have determined developments in the past, and how important was each of them?,
(d) what developments can be expected in the future provided that the same factors with the same quantitative effects determine them?

The former questions, (a) and (c), are more or less the same in both approaches, but the latter questions, (b) and (d), differ markedly. While under the conventional approach the factors that have governed past developments are supposed to go on doing so in the future (with the same quantitative effects, too), under the alternative approach advocated here it is assumed that future developments will be determined by different sets of variables. The basic problem then is not so much to predict future values of known exogenous variables as to predict what new variables will enter the picture, what old ones will lose their effect, and what will be the quantitative influence of new and remaining old variables.

To what errors the "naïve" approach could lead becomes clear when an effort is made to "forecast" the present by using, for example, information available up to 1965, thus leaving out of account the economic recession due to the oil crisis, the plummeting birth rate, and the increasing weight attached in recent years to environmental factors. In that way we should neglect not only any new factors that have entered the picture but also the spectacular increase in the quantitative effects of certain variables that before 1965 hardly counted. Obviously, such a forecast would be worthless, and just as obviously it would be naïve to assume that by now, in the year 1979, all the big changes are behind us, and that from now on regional scientists may base their forecasts on a stable set of variables with known influences. Like it or not, the set of variables will continue to change in the future as it has in the past. This is, indeed, a *fundamental* problem of forecasting, and, therefore, of regional and urban policy-makers who wish to incorporate dynamic factors in their regional and urban policy. Indeed, on the urban and regional levels it is even harder to make predictions than on the national level, the information on and understanding of recent developments being comparatively meagre and unsatisfactory.

Too much time elapses before any statistics come available, and they are inadequate anyway. The information is often already outdated before we use it, and we risk basing our forecasts on sets of variables not even representative of developments in recent years.

Ignorance of the problems indicated in the former paragraphs may well have caused urban policy in the context of regional policy to fail so manifestly in several countries of Western Europe. Up till today it has been assumed that the larger urban areas were the prosperous regions *par excellence*, and that any measure aimed at slowing down their growth would benefit not only the urban regions themselves but also all other regions, for they would be the recipients of the urban areas' overspill. What was mostly overlooked were some basic factors already at work in the larger agglomerations, factors that would justify their being listed among the "potentially depressed" rather than among the "prosperous" regions. The signs had been there for years but they were mostly ignored, and still are in some cases. Moreover, the governments, having committed themselves to support recognized depressed regions, just were not ready for a policy change.

The "factors at work" have already been referred to earlier; it seems worth our while to highlight some of them.

First of all, it is evident that environmental considerations are increasingly influencing the behaviour of families. People in Western Europe are leaving the large agglomerations where their environment is deteriorating all the time for medium-sized towns which offer a more pleasant environment, in the widest sense. And although there is no statistical evidence of potential migrants *to* urban agglomerations changing their motives, it may safely be assumed that these motives point in the same directions as those of the emigrants. Both tendencies together resulted in an increasing out-migration, which soon approached and sometimes exceeded the natural population growth.

The process was accelerated by factors influencing birth and death rates. The dramatic fall in the birth rate due to the improvement and widespread use of contraceptives had, of course, a direct effect on the rate of natural population growth; this was reinforced by an indirect effect: the higher average age of the population caused the death rate to go up. Together with the negative migration rate these two effects are in an increasing number of the larger Western European agglomerations (with more than 200,000 inhabitants) resulting in a negative population growth. Belgium, the United Kingdom, and the Netherlands are the most striking examples, but there are clear signs that similar developments are imminent in France and also in the Federal Republic of Germany. In the present study of urban developments in fourteen Western and Eastern European countries in the period between 1950 and 1975, statistical evidence on that score will become available. In this study, all municipalities with a commuting rate of over 15 per cent of their working population towards the central city of the agglomeration are considered to belong to that agglomeration.

Besides demographic factors, economic and social factors started to influence the development of agglomerations. As economic growth was slowing down, the national total of job opportunities first remained stable and then in some cases began to decrease. Relocation of activities from major agglomerations to other regions, in particular to medium-sized towns, much advocated and even stimulated by government measures, overshot its mark by not just checking the feverish growth of total employment in these agglomerations, but actually reducing, in absolute terms, the number of job opportunities there. Although lagging a few years behind the population decline, the employment decline is no less evident. There is little doubt that it actually follows from the population decline, and more specifically from the fact that it is the financially stronger citizens who leave. However, the employment exodus may also be looked upon as an autonomous phenomenon, involving in particular activities in the service sector. For such activities, large agglomerations are not necessarily the best locations; indeed, a city of minor importance with cheap facilities readily available and plenty of space for expansion might serve equally well, if not better.

In addition, the changed attitude of women towards their participation in the labour force autonomously increased the supply of female workers, and thus added, directly or indirectly, to the number of unemployed. Indeed, what with the expansion of the female labour force and the economic recession, the absolute number of unemployed people in urban areas has come to exceed by far that in the so-called depressed areas. In the Netherlands, for example, there are far more unemployed in the West—the urban areas—than in the traditionally depressed areas of the North, although, admittedly, relative unemployment level is still lower.

The process we just described differs fundamentally from the one described earlier. There we blamed the unfortunate, often one-sided employment structure in certain regions for their depressed state; under the circumstances, the introduction of employment opportunities in new, growing sectors in sufficient number and diversity was the obvious remedy. The philosophy behind the growth-pole concept—the growth of one sector induces growth in others, and together they create an income effect that in turn will give new impulses to all sectors—was certainly applicable to those regions. If they were aided in building up a diversified growing economy, they would from a certain point onwards be able to sustain their own growth without outside help.

The process now observed in the Western European formerly prosperous areas, the large agglomerations, is not one of self-sustained growth, but rather one of self-sustained contraction. Large agglomerations have become poles of contraction existing side by side and interacting with growth poles. The more successful the growth poles, the faster the contraction in the large agglomerations, and vice versa.

The situation in Eastern European countries is different. The larger agglomerations there are still growing at considerable speed and find themselves in a position where both the core city of the agglomeration and the ring municipalities around the core increase in population and employment. The largest agglomerations among these, however, the primate cities, are in a somewhat different position. There, development shows already signs of suburbanization, sometimes still *in statu nescendi*, sometimes quite manifest, for instance in the case of Hungary and Poland where a number of cities have left the stage of urbanization behind and clearly entered the next stage, that of suburbanization.

The comparison of urban development in Western and Eastern Europe suggests that although "innovative" factors do play an important role, there is a basic logic in the process of urban development, in the sense that the sequences of stages is governed by the internal dynamics of the urban system. Urban growth is followed by urban sprawl, which ends in urban decline. Whether urban decline will be followed by reurbanization, by a revival of the city, is a question that is very hard to answer. The possibility that the system, either through its internal dynamics or indirectly through corrective government measures, moves in that direction should certainly not be excluded. In the city of Rotterdam a distinct reurbanization policy is pursued; it is too early yet to say whether it will be successful.

The developments through time go hand in hand with developments in space. When we described the situation in Western European larger agglomerations, we already pointed out that while all these agglomerations are gradually entering the stage of urban decline, of desurbanization, other cities, smaller in size and situated in more pleasant surroundings, are growing and flourishing. The international pattern, suggesting that the level of economic development determines the stage of urban development in which the larger agglomerations find themselves, seems to repeat itself on the national level, where some (large) cities are declining and other (medium-sized) cities are growing. The developments on the national level are by no means due to regional differences in economic development, however. The better quality of life in the smaller cities seems much more decisive here, and it may even be that economic development in many medium-sized towns in Western Europe is the result rather than the cause of their attractiveness as residences.

The foregoing considerations all point towards one conclusion: growth and decline go hand in hand. A fact we are all familiar with as far as sectors are concerned. We also know that the sectoral evolution is reflected in regional evolution, favourable to some areas, unfavourable to others. Regional developments used to be the consequence of sectoral developments. Now it seems that the tide has turned, and that in highly urbanized regions the sectoral developments have become dependent on the regional ones. The decreasing population there, the unwillingness to live and work in the larger cities, have become basic locational factors, making for reduced employment, which in turn reinforces the tendency towards decline. The sectoral developments have shifted to other regions, more favoured by workers as places to live and work in.

In the past, the decline of one sector in a region could to a degree be compensated by the growth of other sectors in the same region. Regional decline, on the contrary, is only quasi-compensated on the national level by growth in other regions, a poor consolation for the urban regions hit by decline. And for any reurbanization policy to restore the balance with the help of proper measures, we must rely on a shaky theory and scarce, already outdated, information on the factors that in the national poles of contraction, that is, in the larger agglomerations, work towards desurbanization. The recognition of that fact does not leave us much room for optimism, but it does justify the existence of our discipline and the efforts we make to enhance our knowledge.

It also justifies the undertaking in urban research called CURB of which the present volume reflects the findings of the first stage. CURB stands for Costs of Urban Growth and is the name of a project coordinated by the Center of Documentation and Coordination of Research in Social Sciences in Vienna. It aims at making a study in which, on the one hand, urban development in countries with different signatures are compared and, on the other hand, developments over time are studied on the national and on the regional level. The incorporation of the temporal as well as the spatial dimension in urban developments is the main characteristic of the CURB project.

It is difficult to describe the ultimate goal of the CURB project more precisely. Urban developments are a reflection of societal developments and manifest themselves in all fields of human behaviour. Economic developments, social changes, environmental factors, transportation and finance all play their role in determining the development of the urban system. They are all interrelated and have all of them a temporal and a spatial dimension. It is the intention that all these fields will be studied on an international comparative basis as well as on an interregional national basis. The actual execution of the programme of studies for the future cannot be forecast very accurately and has to evolve in the course of time. It cannot be described precisely but it may suffice to have indicated here the main fields into which future studies will have to penetrate.

The present volume consists of three parts. In the first a *theory* of urban developments is presented. Its main feature is a description of the factors that are, in the opinion of the authors, to be held responsible for the transitions from one stage of urban development to the next. It, moreover, suggests that the larger the city and the higher its level of economic development, the closer the city finds itself to the stage of desurbanization, the stage in which the agglomeration as a whole starts to decline.

The theoretical part is followed by Part II in which the results of the statistical testing of part of the theory are presented. For that purpose statistical data on a large number of urban agglomerations in fourteen countries collected by the national teams were available. It seems that broadly speaking the results of the analysis of the data confirm the theory presented in the first part and that the concepts introduced there could be used efficiently in the testing. It appeared, moreover, that the progress of national urban systems along the urbanization–suburbanization–desurbanization road accelerated dramatically during the period 1970–1975, the most recent period that was taken into consideration.

The third part is dedicated to urban policy. It presents a theory of urban policy as well as an evaluation of national urban policies in the fourteen countries studied. Its main finding is that urban policy in fact has never been corrective but has practically always promoted the transition from one stage to another. It has been, as such, endogenous to the dynamics of the development of the urban system. It was not exogenous in the sense that it was steering the urban system in a given, explicitly described, direction. Only recently here and there measures can be traced that try to check the trend towards decline, but they seem to come solely from individual city governments and not (yet) from national governments.

A very important question is what benefits governments can derive from the results of this study. The benefits could be that they are forewarned of what the future has in store for them, so that they can take timely measures to mitigate the harmful consequences of autonomous developments. Hopefully their urban policy might even wax powerful enough to break through the dynamics of the system and actually to check the downward progress towards desurbanization.

For the participants in the study of European urban development there could be no greater reward for their intensive common effort than that governments responsible for urban policy in Eastern and Western Europe would start to reconsider the objectives of their policy, critically evaluate the instruments to be used and work together to achieve one general objective: to make Europe a better place to live and work in. The need to develop better steering mechanism has never been so urgent as now that the very existence of the economic, social, and cultural centres of our nation is at stake.

As was already mentioned before, this volume reflects the general findings of the first stage of the investigation. More results of this stage will be presented in forthcoming volumes.

PART I

Elements of a Theory of Urban Development

1

Introduction

Among contemporary trends, urbanization is almost unanimously looked upon as one of the most drastic.

Progressive urbanization such as we observe nowadays is a recent phenomenon. For thousands of years there have been towns, or at any rate certain forms of concentrated settlement, but only in about the last century and a half have we witnessed such a massive growth in urban population. The process started in Europe and was taken up in other parts of the Northern hemisphere; nowadays, the most impressive urbanization processes are taking place in developing countries. However, as this book sets out to compare urban development and governmental urban policy within fourteen European countries in the post-war period, we shall focus our attention predominantly on developments in Europe.

In Part I, the spatial changes that occur in various urbanization patterns will be discussed in a general way and the desirability of certain developments will be considered from a policy point of view. The particular point we wish to include is whether the present spatial development of urban systems is the optimum one, the one that people desire.

The present stage of urban development at which the European countries involved in our comparison find themselves can be denoted by one of the following expressions: depopulation of rural areas—expansion of towns and building of new ones—formation of agglomerations—suburbanization—decline of old city centres—etc. Each of these key trends indicates a complex of spatial changes and a corresponding set of problems which confront policy-makers. Many urban problems result from discrepancies between the physical, constructed elements—houses, industrial buildings, streets, roads, railways—and the use that people who live and work in an urban area make of them.

Because physical elements represent large investments and can have a long lifespan, they cannot be adapted instantly to suit new requirements and new modes of use. In the meantime, however, there will be friction and

3

congestion, causing all manner of problems: the problems of sub-optimum spatial development.

In Chapters 2, 3, and 9 an attempt will be made to set up a general theoretical framework within which to study such problems with a view to pointing the way towards the optimum spatial development of towns.

To that end, it will be assumed that there is a connection between a country's urban-development stage as indicated by one of the key expressions listed above and its socio-economic development stage. More specifically, our starting-point will be that every development stage has its own characteristic urbanization pattern. Of course, we cannot go so far as to maintain that a country which passes from one socio-economic development stage to another, "higher" one will automatically assume the corresponding urbanization pattern; in fact, at any stage of socio-economic development, appropriate urban policy can only change urban development as far as physical and technical constraints (among them transport facilities) will allow.

What is to be understood by urbanization?

There are still many who associate the notion of urbanization exclusively with the way people live: either dispersed across space in a large number of smallish nuclei, or concentrated in larger, densely populated towns. However, urbanization refers quite as much to the way people work, spend their leisure time, communicate with one another, and bridge distances. The settlement pattern existing at a given moment is the consequence of all these factors, and cannot be ascribed to changes in housing patterns alone.

In Eastern Europe the term urbanization is used both in urban and in regional studies and in practical regional planning to denote two essentially different phenomena. In the older or traditional approach, which roughly reflected theory and practice until the Second World War, urbanization comprises the phenomena associated with the development of towns and of the urban population. In many European countries this is still the most common approach to practical regional planning.

This traditional concept of urbanization, however, is no longer adequate. Urbanization has acquired new features in many countries. The following four are the most important.

1. The continuing concentration of economic and social life and of the population in growth poles of different sizes. This process was generated by the economics of scale inherent in industrial manufacture and in services, and is also the result of technological progress in production and transport as well as of the individual's preference for particular places of residence and work (better job opportunities and better housing prospects, accessibility to specialized services, etc.).

2. The spatial and functional integration of neighbouring settlement units or of groupings of such units, which was generated by economic cooperation, higher social mobility, and the development of communication systems.

3. Parallel to this, the deconcentration of socio-economic life in settlement units or settlement groupings. This process stemmed from rising living standards, the expansion of urban transport and infrastructure, and private car ownership, as well as the need to allocate sites for the expansion of industrial plants and transport facilities.

4. The decrease in the differences in living standards between rural and urban areas

through a gradual assimilation by the rural population of an urban life style, its work patterns, dwelling arrangements, recreational pursuits and services.

These processes manifest themselves in Eastern Europe mainly by:

—changes in housing construction in the rural areas as well as in the provision of rural housing and rural settlements with urban-type services,

—the growing number of nonagricultural jobs in typically rural areas; depending on the economic level the given country has reached, industrial or service jobs predominate,

—changes in the occupational structure of the rural population, which becomes increasingly nonagricultural. Because of the increase in nonagricultural job opportunities this change embraces all the rural areas; it is particularly apparent in areas within commuting distance of agglomerations and towns.

The processes mentioned above under points 1–3 generate a transformation in the spatial structure of urban settlements. At present new growth poles emerge more and more frequently not in cities with high spatial concentration but in less congested groupings of spatial-functional structures—the urban agglomerations. Thus the processes of urbanization as they occur in recent times can be said to involve:

1. a further increase in urban population and the development of existing towns as well as the emergence of new ones;

2. the transformation of compact towns into more loosely connected groupings of settlement units—urban agglomerations;

3. the spatial-functional integration of neighbouring urban agglomerations;

4. the urbanization of typically rural areas.

The urbanization processes, complex as they are, result in a great diversity of spatial forms; equally diverse are the ways in which urbanization affects the transformation of regional structures.

The form, scope and rate of urbanization depends on the level of socio-economic development attained, the geographic conditions, and the institutional structures of the given country and on the preferences of individual population groups, authorities, enterprises, and other factors participating in the processes of socio-economic development.

The various urbanization processes in the countries of Eastern Europe have certain characteristic features that distinguish them from analogous developments in Western Europe. There are several reasons for this, one of the most important being that in the East urbanization started later than in the West, and hence took place in a different social, economic and technological context. In the last thirty years the process here has been shaped by forces such as the social ownership of the means of production and of a system of planned economy, as well as the varying degrees of governmental and managerial decentralization.[1]

We will investigate the extent to which the three factors, viz. different stages of development, different degrees of planned intervention, and different social and technological conditions, have influenced actual developments in different countries and regions. It is not *a priori* certain that developments in socialist countries have led or rather will lead to cities of a different social, economic, and physical structure than in countries with a market economy. However, it is to be expected that although the general structure may be similar, specific features appear in Eastern European countries more or less often than in Western European countries, depending on the degree to which the government has intervened in actual developments.

[1] From *Elements of a Theory of Urbanization Processes in Socialist Countries* by S. Herman and J. Regulski, Vienna Centre, WD 3/77.

Whether it takes place in Eastern or in Western Europe, in socialist countries or in countries with a market economy, there is no doubt that urbanization is a very complicated and highly dynamic process.

If urbanization is conceived of as a complex, interdependent process, then urban policy must be visualized as multidimensional. Urban policy, if it is to give guidance in effecting changes in the spatial settlement pattern, needs to affect all the factors underlying that pattern.

An integrated policy approach to urbanization must therefore be concerned with all aspects of urbanization: the location of places of employment, structure of employment, traffic and transport, construction of infrastructure, supply of public services and welfare facilities, and the environment. In actual practice, these various aspects often come under the responsibility of different government ministries, who develop separate policies for them. In that case, in view of the integrated nature of the urbanization process, urban policy must first and foremost seek to coordinate the efforts of all the individual administrative bodies that influence urban settlements.

A similar requirement holds for regional and national policy too. For—and this is another assumption—national, regional, and urban policy are by no means independent entities. Each of them implies the others, and they cannot be effective unless working fully in harmony. Problems are taken up at different administrative levels not so much because they have different effects as that they are perceived differently. The construction of a national system of motoways on behalf of the national government, for instance, influences what happens at a local level, and, on the other hand, the allocation of a local industrial site by a municipal government affects the use that is made of the system of motorways.

In Chapters 2, 3, and 9 a conceptual framework will be set up which takes into account the complex and dynamic character of the urbanization process, and deals with urban change and urban policy as parts of an intergated whole. Two approaches will be made. First in Chapters 2 and 3 an attempt will be made to collect elements for a general theory of the spatial changes in urban patterns, as a framework against which to judge the actual spatial change of towns. Such a theory will have to be general enough to be valid for developments in both Eastern and Western Europe with their different political systems, different stages of urban development and different socio-economic and technological conditions in which the process of urbanization evolved.

In formulating this theory, assumptions will be made about the way individuals and collectives behave when they try, with the help of the tools available to them, to realize their objectives. This part of the theory reflects a kind of social philosophy based on considerations of welfare theory, with, as an added dimension, the role that space plays in people's pursuit of welfare.

Against the background of this philosophy the second approach is taken through which, to show up urban development and the hand government has in it, different stages of urban development are defined and a broad review of actual historical events is given. For each stage, the main spatial developments and the urban problems attending them are pointed out.

Chapter 9 dealing with the kind of urban policies which are available to the government is linked to the first welfare-theoretical part of this book, in that a model of the urban system is formulated on the basis of these general considerations.

We hope to have shown in this way how urban change and urban policy are integral parts of urban functioning, and which interrelationships and pre-conditions have to be considered before urban systems can be directed towards a state approaching the optimum, that is, for the greatest welfare of their inhabitants.

2

The Actors in the Urban System

A general theory of the spatial changes in urban systems must necessarily take into account behaviour of the various actors in the process of urban change, and explain how and according to what assumptions that behaviour leads to the spatial changes observed. The ultimate aim of such a theory is to derive from a study of the actors' behaviour, and from a logical sequence of casual relations, a meaningful explanation of relevant spatial developments. In order to lay the foundations for such a theory, this section intends to give a qualitative survey of the various points of view from which the modern problems of urban change and urban policy could be dealt with; to present a kind of philosophy, a kind of background against which urban development and the part government plays in it can be made understandable. This philosophy is based on elements of welfare theory, into which the dimension of space in people's pursuit of welfare will be incorporated. Thus, a spatial welfare function will be defined for each actor, and it will be demonstrated that spatial changes in urban systems can be seen as the result of people's actions and reactions as they endeavour to realize a welfare-objective set. We do not pretend to offer a fully fledged theory of spatial behaviour, but we do hope to establish the basis for such a theory.

2.1. Households as actors in the urban system

Households—families with children—and also households of single people or aged persons, and other kinds of co-habitation—are the first actors we shall discuss.

They can be the inhabitants of a town, a region, or a country, according to the level on which the study focuses. From a spatial point of view, the behaviour of households is composed of a large number of decisions about

8

the location of residences or places of work, the services and amenities which, given home and work locations, people want to and can have available, and the way in which they travel between home, work, and amenities.

It has been assumed that choosing a residence is a household's primary decision; and that other decisions are made in relation to the point in space where the household is domiciled. From that point, certain jobs may be considered to be within commuting distance for the economically active members of the family, while others may be thought too far. Within access of the residence, individual members of the household will demand the usual provisions, such as shops, schools, hospitals, churches, welfare services, parks, sports facilities, etc.

The patterns that emerge indicate that decisions made by households are affected in many ways by the behaviour of other actors: other households as well as private or public industries, which provide employment, and governments, which provide services. There is, for one thing, a clear interdependence between the location of residential areas and that of employment. People will want to live where there is employment or where employment is expected to increase in the near future; on the other hand, industries will want to establish themselves where there is an adequate supply of labour. In households where more than one member has a job, the location decision can be very complex. While one family member may have taken himself closer to his work by moving to a new residence, other members may find themselves living farther away from their jobs. It must be assumed that households internally reach a unanimous preference-ordering concerning their location decisions, and that they behave as a unity.

In order to give substance, in a more systematic way, to the interdependence observed, we shall assume that each actor's behaviour is goal-oriented and can be described in terms of an objective function. This approach is known from the theory of consumers' and producers' behaviour in traditional economics, which is based on the objective of maximizing either welfare or profits. Two objections can be raised in either case: first, to the fact that only one criterion is applied—however broadly formulated as far as consumers are concerned in terms of the utility obtained from the consumption of goods and services—and second, to the complete absence of the spatial aspect.

Indeed, a person's (and a household's) welfare is determined not only by the goods and services they consume, but also by the environment in which they do so. Recent discussion about the quality of life in relation to the pollution of the environment has revealed that, after material goods and services, people's well-being depends on clean air, a park to walk in, pleasant surroundings to live in, and easily accessible public facilities.

Obviously, the places providing these things are essential; hence, the spatial element naturally introduces itself into consumer theory. It is impossible for everybody to have every amenity near at hand; most of them will be at some distance from the user, who will have to bridge that distance to enjoy them. Transport implies cost, time and effort, all of which have to be weighed against the satisfaction gained from using the amenities. A drastic way to gain access to specific facilities located at a considerable distance is, of course, moving house; in that case, the pros and cons of the old and new places of residence will have to be carefully weighed before the decision is made. We shall come back to this aspect later.

On the supposition that the objective a household pursues is an improvement in its welfare, it seems worth while to take a closer look at the welfare concept and in particular its spatial dimension, a central point in the present argument.

Welfare, in the wide sense indicated earlier, comprises not only the availability of material goods and services (possibly represented by income level or job status), but also that of less measurable items such as the atmosphere at home and at work, the attractiveness of one's living environment, the presence of a social infrastructure, the means available to a household to bridge the distances between home and the location of certain welfare components.

It may be assumed that a person's feeling of well-being always depends on a *combination* of welfare components. Now the combinations found in some places will be better or richer than those found elsewhere, and the difference makes for welfare discrepancies between households at various locations. But even with equal combinations there may still be discrepancies, for different people have preferences for different welfare components. A nature-loving person who lives in beautiful surroundings where income prospects are only moderate may well be just as happy as someone who lives in a less beautiful but economically stronger region. Individual preference ranking is denoted as a *preference* or *welfare function*, indicating the weights attributed to the welfare components in a certain combination by the subject or household concerned.

Now let us first consider the spatial dimension of each welfare component, indicating the effect of location and accessibility. Because transport costs represent a sacrifice, it may be assumed that a facility near at hand contributes more to well-being than a similar facility farther away. In regional science the concept of "potential" is used to express the relevant spatial relationship.

By weighting similar facilities or amenities at various places with distance costs, a potential can indicate the extent to which such amenities or facilities are accessible from a user's location. For example, a townsman's recreation potential can be shown in the form of a variable indicating the degree to which recreation areas, both near his home town and farther away, are at his disposal, given the distances to these areas, and the costs in money, time and inconvenience needed to bridge those distances. By integrating potentials, and hence the spatial element, in a welfare function, a *spatial welfare function* can be obtained which describes how each welfare potential contributes to a household's well-being.

Let us assume, for the sake of convenience, that people's well-being is determined by three components, chosen, among other reasons, because they are relevant to the discussion of the spatial development of urban systems, viz.

—a *housing potential*, referring not only to the house but also to its surroundings: the quality of its environment, green spaces, etc.;
—a *working potential*, standing for the availability of jobs as well as for their differentiation and attendant income differences; and
—an *amenities potential*, representing the availability of shops, education, health care, culture, recreational activities, social welfare, religion, etc.

Obviously such a framework is not quite realistic, because it disregards the problems of actually aggregating the countless welfare potentials of real life into the three mentioned above. However, as a guide to the understanding of urban processes, it will do.

It is common practice to define in relation to the tension, or discrepancy, between needs and available means, or, more accurately: welfare can be determined by the degree to which needs are satisfied by means. The proportion in which the various welfare components contribute to the level of welfare experienced depends on the relative urgency of the needs for these components, i.e. on subjective preferences for, respectively, housing, employment, and amenities, to keep within the terminology of our framework. We may say, then, that welfare is determined simultaneously by the ratios between the actual and desired levels of the various potentials, each weighted by coefficients that represent the individual household's relative preference for each of them.

A welfare function expressing welfare as discussed above can be defined tentatively in more formal terms as:

$$W_i = \left(\frac{\Pi_{hi}}{\Pi_{hi}^*}\right)^{\alpha_h} \left(\frac{\Pi_{wi}}{\Pi_{wi}^*}\right)^{\alpha_w} \left(\frac{\Pi_{vi}}{\Pi_{vi}^*}\right)^{\alpha_v} \qquad (2.1)$$

in which W_i is the welfare level of a household in region i, and Π_{hi}, Π_{wi} and Π_{vi} are the various potentials in i (Π^* being the desired potentials or aspiration levels), defined as:

$$\Pi_{hi} = \sum_{j=1}^{J} x_j^h \, e^{-\delta^h c_{ij}^h} \tag{2.2}$$

in which:

x_j^h = size of facility h in region j, weighted by some quality index $(x = s.q)$;

$e^{-\delta^h c_{ij}^h}$ = a specification of a distance function, in which c_{ij}^h represents the generalized transport costs, determined as the weighted sum of all costs, in money, time, and effort, of bridging the distance, and δ^h is a coefficient representing the sensitivity to distance of this specific facility h.

The task of quantifying the first three elements is a formidable one, but inventiveness might overcome the main difficulties, thus creating the opportunity for us to analyse and judge a particular situation in a city on a much broader basis than has been possible so far in most cases. Still, even if this task were fulfilled, two more problems would remain to be solved. First, the welfare level of an urban population depends, not only on the first three variables, but also on the aspiration levels of that population. The second problem, closely linked to the first, relates to the fact that government policy usually treats each of the three above-mentioned elements separately. We will deal with the former problem in this section, and with the latter problem in Part III.

If we assume as an introductory hypothesis that the aspiration level of the population equals the maximum level found in the country, (2.1) becomes

$$W_i = \left(\frac{\Pi_{hi}}{\Pi_h^{\max}} \right)^{\alpha^h} \left(\frac{\Pi_{wi}}{\Pi_w^{\max}} \right)^{\alpha^w} \left(\frac{\Pi_{vi}}{\Pi_v^{\max}} \right)^{\alpha^v}. \tag{2.3}$$

Such a formal presentation may seem somewhat dubious at first, but does, in fact, come fairly close to the actual situation. People tend to compare their level of well-being in each respect with the maximum level reached in their country and maybe even in other countries with which they are familiar. This implies that their well-being will decrease as they are becoming better informed about the situation elsewhere. One might call this the destructive influence of communication. It also implies that people's well-being decreases as the situation in the best region or city improves further, even if from an "objective" point of view their overall situation becomes better. We could formalize this statement by writing

$$J_i = \left(\frac{\Pi_h^{\max} - \Pi_{hi}}{\Pi_{hi}} \right)^{\beta^h} \left(\frac{\Pi_w^{\max} - \Pi_{wi}}{\Pi_{wi}} \right)^{\beta^w} \left(\frac{\Pi_v^{\max} - \Pi_{vi}}{\Pi_{vi}} \right)^{\beta^v} \tag{2.4}$$

as the "jealousy" function explaining dissatisfaction as a function of the relative deficits felt in each main element of welfare.

This function shares a number of interesting features with (2.3). If the maxima of the Π's are all found in one urban region, all the elements of (2.3) are equal to unity there, and for as long as this region manages to maintain its position, its population will never experience an increase in well-being. It will have become a constant, whatever happens in the actual situation. By the same token all elements of (2.4) become zero, so there is no "jealousy". Well-being is constant, jealousy is absent; the situation is stable.

Another interesting feature is that the well-being in a region remains constant if the elements of its functions increase in proportion to the maxima of these elements; in that case there is neither increase in well-being, nor decrease in "jealousy".

A third feature is that since generally the maxima will *not* all be found in the same region, each region has a feeling of being worsted in comparison to other regions even if its total welfare in an objective sense is maximum. If, for instance, for a given region

$$\varphi_i = \varphi_i(\Pi_{hi}, \Pi_{wi}, \Pi_{vi}) \tag{2.5}$$

would be higher than in any other region because of a very high level of Π_{hi}, w_i might still be lower, because, for instance, there is one region where Π_w^{max} is much higher than in the region under consideration, and another where Π_v^{max} is higher.

If that is true, we cannot be optimistic about the possibility of increasing well-being in our cities. Rising aspirations prevent people from becoming satisfied, and when they have reached the maximum in all respects a final, constant level of well-being will prevail, no matter what further developments take place.

If there were some kind of objective concept of well-being by which two regions could find themselves in equal positions even if the different elements of their well-being showed different values, the government could disregard the arguments put forward by the population with regard to one element, pointing at the compensation afforded by another element. If, however, such a function does not exist, the government has no such way out. Instead, it will have to shift to a policy that conforms to function (2.4), trying to fill the gap in each element in each urban region. A considerable amount of money will then have to be spent on raising levels of provision that, even in regions where from an "objective" point of view well-being is maximum, are below the corresponding levels in other regions.

People in regions with high-level amenities and excellent job opportunities will require from the government that the environmental quality of their region is improved and becomes as good as in the region with the highest environmental status. Regions with high-level amenities and excellent environmental qualities will urge for improvement in the quality and quantity of jobs available in the region, etc.

Whatever measure is taken, it cannot improve the level of well-being of the country as a whole unless the speed at which the level of the different elements in the non-maximum regions is raised exceeds that in the maximum regions. Absolute increases are uninteresting, only relative improvements exceeding the relative improvements in the "best" levels count.

An optimal governmental welfare policy, however, requires among other things that the government is aware of the fact that a certain trade-off between welfare components can exist. Only then can an optimal allocation of means over regions and functions be achieved. In the Mathematical Appendix this argument has been worked out. At this stage we will not go into any further detail concerning this point but concentrate rather on another aspect of the welfare function, viz. that it differs in structure for different socio-economic groups of the population.

The objective function (2.1) applies to individual households in general. It is more realistic, however, to identify more or less *homogeneous groups* of households showing conformity in spatial behaviour and in the environmental qualities they require. Such groups could be defined according to such socio-economic criteria as age, social status, income, or education. For each of these groups a welfare function can be specified, distinguished from others by the weighting assigned to the various welfare potentials; obviously, one socio-economic group of households may value employment more than environment, while another group's preferences may be just the opposite.

After discussing the other actors in Sections 2.2 and 2.3, the concepts of objective function, welfare component, and potential will be used in Chapter 3 in an attempt to explain the development of urban structures as the collective result of the goal-oriented behaviour of all the actors involved. It has been assumed that individual households as well as groups of households will try by their behaviour to maximize their well-being. We shall see in what follows that important spatial developments, such as the shifting of residential areas and the phenomena of commuting and migration, and hence the growth of cities and the evolution of their structure, can be described as expressions of attempts at welfare maximization. People will strive for a location that is optimum in relation to the distribution of potentials across the urban area, given the quality of the transport system.

The transport system is indeed of paramount importance, because transport facilities directly determine the accessibility of welfare components.

The development of motorized transport frees households from the need to choose a residential location which brings work and home as close together as possible. The better the transport system—public and private—the less reason there is for households to object to living at a distance from work places and from elements of social infrastructure. By becoming commuters, people can realize their preferences for certain residential qualities and still enjoy the advantages offered by urban concentrations. This is how the phenomenon of suburbanization comes into being.

A more static approach is possible, of course. If, given the location of the various potentials, households want to increase their welfare without moving to other areas, they can do so by efforts to raise the quality, volume, or accessibility of welfare components at their disposal on the spot. Now improving and increasing potentials as we have defined them is in many cases the responsibility of the government, which thus provides for the preferences of the citizens it governs. It does happen, however, that potentials are raised as the result of action by individuals, private organizations, or industries, sometimes guided or supported by the government.

In Sections 2.2 and 2.3, the roles played by industries and public authorities as actors in the urban system will be discussed.

2.2. The industrial sector as an actor in the urban system

It is now the turn of the powerful industrial sector to come under scrutiny, seeking to realize its own objectives, either within a national plan or independently.

We have already seen that the welfare level of households is largely determined by potentials relating to the availability of jobs. Indeed, the spatial distribution of employment is one of the determining factors in the locational behaviour of households, and consequently of the spatial development of urban systems.

The distribution of employment across a country results from the spatial actions of industries or relevant government ministries. Again we shall investigate how choices of location made by them can be explained by their or the government's objectives, what the dominant factors are, and what response they make to changing conditions. In order to clarify how industrial locational behaviour affects urban evolution, special attention will be given to the significance of towns as industrial locations.

Industries play an important role not only by creating employment, but also because they affect the provisions potential, inasmuch as their final products represent provisions for the population. The term "industries" should be understood here to include institutions like corporate organizations which play an important part in the development of such urban facilities as office buildings, shopping centres, and housing schemes.

On the other hand, the establishment of an industry may have negative consequences in terms of increased traffic congestion, parking problems, environmental nuisance, or increased tension on the labour market. A new establishment can shatter the competitive conditions within a sector to such an extent as to jeopardize the continuity of existing firms. A recent example in Western European countries is the introduction of large retail establishments outside towns, which can have grave consequences for existing small-scale shops within those towns.

Such external effects of the location of industries or services will invoke reactions from the population and also from the government, which is responsible for the fair distribution of the advantages and disadvantages of such developments.

All in all there are ample reasons to treat the industrial sector as playing a separate role in the process of urban change.

2.2.1. *Objectives and locational behaviour*

As for households, the choice of the location of industrial establishments largely determines the extent to which their objectives can be realized. The objective which industries aim at will here be defined as "profitable continuity". Location is important, for an industry must have access to an adequate market in which to sell its products, and be accessible to the inputs required in its production process. To both conditions, the constraint of transportation costs weighing upon the financial results applies.

Differences in supply and demand potentialities between regions, between town and country, between subregions within an urban region, make for differences in the attractiveness of industrial locations. True to its objective, a rational company or government will choose for its industries a location that promises supply and demand at the lowest communication costs. The ultimate choice will depend on the nature of the production process, which may be more or less output- or input-oriented, and on an evaluation of each separate location factor, taking into account future expectations. In extreme cases this evaluation procedure may lead to a location decision based entirely either on demand or on supply factors; the corner-shop for daily necessities represents a fair example of a fully demand-oriented location decision.

From the foregoing it follows that the town is the ideal location for activities depending, whether for their sales or for their input requirements, on the urban milieu, which offers a spatial concentration of buyers and labour in adequate variety, as well as all kinds of agglomeration economies in terms of production, distribution, and communication. In particular for producers of consumer goods, a location in an urban region where people and purchasing power are concentrated is to be preferred. The establishment of the peripheral retail stores referred to earlier in connection with external effects, however, demonstrates the considerable influence on the evolution of the spatial location pattern that is exerted by improved transport facilities, both for industrial establishments and for their customers.

Industries for which the supply of inputs is of primary importance are less likely to be attracted to urban locations, unless they are highly dependent on the specific kinds of labour and the personal contacts and sources of information available only in cities.

In the majority of cases a company's locational behaviour will be determined by a mixture of supply and demand considerations, which can be seen as primary and secondary location factors. In subsection 2.2.2 industrial locational behaviour will be analysed in more detail with the help of the terminology introduced in Section 2.1.

2.2.2. *Demand and supply potentials*

The application of the concept of potentials to the analysis of locational behaviour offers similar advantages in this case as in that of individual residential choice. Indeed, the attractiveness of a region or town as a location for an economic activity is determined by the availability of elements that are needed for the production process—raw materials and auxiliaries, labour, services, customers, and facilities for the transport of all these elements. It is not necessary for the elements to be present in an industry's own region; distances can be bridged, and the industry may potentially obtain its input from, and sell its products to, all other regions. The actual range of the area relevant to an industry depends on the influence of distance and the associated transport and communication costs. The effect of the level of demand and supply factors in surrounding regions on a certain region's attractiveness as an area of location diminishes as the distances to be bridged and the communication costs increase, a phenomenon that is adequately expressed in the "potential".

The foregoing implies that locational behaviour consists of an assessment of the *demand and supply potentials* of a number of alternative locations, and finally making a choice of whichever location holds out the best prospects for the industry to achieve its goal of maximum profitable continuity. In other words, an industry's objective function is composed of all relevant demand and supply potentials.

Like households, industries can be classified into *homogeneous groups* according to the dominant characteristics of their locational requirements. A group of industries will be comprised of firms whose requirements as to the spatial profile of location factors are similar, and whose valuations of relevant supply and demand potentials are approximately equal. It will then be possible to formulate a specific objective function for each group, distinguished by the group-specific valuation of the potentials. The criteria applied enabled us to ascertain which groups of industries have dominant preferences for the urban milieu: it is those groups that help to decide the development of the spatial pattern of towns.

A *supply potential* of a certain industry in a certain region is defined as the weighted sum over all regions of an input component, the weights representing the generalized transport costs. Inputs consist of raw materials and auxiliaries, capital goods, intermediary services, and, to some extent, labour. It is the labour factor in particular that stimulates companies to settle in towns, where the labour supply is not only plentiful but also diversified in skills, in other words, where one can easily find the kind of labour that elsewhere could only be recruited at a high cost.

Other factors which contribute to the attraction of towns are information, personal contacts, agglomeration economies, and positive external effects, all of them more abundant in urban regions than elsewhere because of the spatial concentration of people and activities.

Obviously, there is a positive correlation between the presence or availability of the elements enumerated above and the urbanization stage of a region. More of them are present in a metropolitan area than in a small regional town; accordingly, activities in the spheres of management, research, and scientific servicing, which to a high degree are attracted by these elements, are to be found first and foremost in large towns, to whose spatial development they contribute in turn.

After the supply potential, the sum of the demand factors, both in the region concerned and in the surrounding areas, is a determining factor of locational behaviour. A *demand potential* can be defined as the weighted sum over all regions of a demand component, the weights again representing the generalized transport costs involved in bridging distances. The presence of buyers of an industry's product is the principal variable in this case. Sales can be divided into (1) final demand from customers and (2) intermediary demand from other industries, either in the production sector or in the distribution sector (trade, shops). Correspondingly, the location of demand-oriented industries may be decided mainly by the presence of, respectively, population concentrations, complexes of other industrial establishments, or business establishments providing for the population. Indeed, the ability of a region or a town to attract demand-oriented industries will depend on the size and composition of the population, its purchasing power, and the complexity of its economic structure, and in an analysis of locational behaviour the stage of urbanization should also be considered as the economic development affects the demand for goods and services and thus the magnitude of demand potentials. It is imperative to take due account of the relationships between location, urbanization, and economic development, particularly in studies undertaken to compare the locational behaviour of industries or Ministries of Industry in different countries.

2.2.3. *The dynamics of industrial behaviour*

An industry will be established at a site where, given all the location factors and taking into account the level of transport and communication costs in particular, it can achieve its objective of profitable continuity to an optimum extent. Obviously expectations about future developments of the principal factors will be a consideration; nevertheless it can happen that a once optimum location for various reasons becomes sub-optimum after a time. Let us examine some of the reasons for this.

(a) Every industry is related in many ways with the location of the population and of other industries; the quality of its location depends on such factors as the population's size, composition, level of training, and income, the nature or volume of production processes, technology, and, to a considerable extent, transport facilities. Changes in these factors constantly call for compensating measures to safeguard the continuity of the firm. Such measures may involve the firm's own trade methods; they may also imply a spatial move to a new location which, given the changed conditions, has become more optimal than the old one.

(b) Establishments in urban regions increasingly have to cope with the problems arising from traffic congestion, which tend to raise communication costs and thus lower the various potentials. Nevertheless, city centres continue to attract new establishments; their demand may send land prices up, causing the city to become in due course a sub-optimum location for firms of older urban standing but which are less productive in relation to the area they occupy.

(c) But even if an area remains virtually the same, it may lose some of its attraction as time goes by, simply because other regions are becoming more accessible as the result of new infrastructure such as a new motorway or rapid transit systems.

Whatever the cause of a location's loss of attraction, spatial relocation may be the necessary action in order that an industry can realize its objectives more effectively.

The reasoning developed above and the examples given emphasize how strongly the relative attractiveness of an industrial location is affected by the spatial–economic behaviour of the other actors in the urban system, particularly because of the countless interrelations within demand and supply potentials. In fact, the locational behaviour of all actors may be arranged in a so-called location chain, with the help of which it is possible to assess how a partial change in one actor's spatial–economic behaviour can affect all the other actors and thus affect the evolution of a town as a whole. Examples of such partial changes have already been mentioned: relocation of the population (and hence of purchasing power) by migration to the suburbs, for instance, and relocation of industries (which may be suppliers as well as customers) under the impact of certain processes of changes. In this respect it must be noted that industries influence urban development not only by means of their locational behaviour. As has already been mentioned, in many Western European countries such industrial groups as building firms, development corporations, and financial institutions influence the spatial allocation of urban investments in such industries as housing, office building, development of shopping and recreational centres, etc. They too share responsibility for the size and quality of urban amenities and thus for the quality of urban life. In general it may be said that the construction industry, like all other industries, primarily tries to achieve continuity. To optimize their investment policy, developers need to know how to allocate their investments, functionally as well as spatially, to their best advantage. To that end, they should acquire information, for instance, about the discrepancies between the actual and the desired quality of housing, the actual and the desired accessibility of facilities such as shops, recreation areas, offices, etc., in every location relevant to them.

Governmental policy can influence, directly or indirectly, the relative attractiveness of a location, and consequently the choice people make of residence and workplace. So it is appropriate to devote Section 2.3 to a discussion of the role of the government as an actor in the urban system. After a general analysis with the help of the set of concepts introduced earlier, urban policy and its instruments will be treated in detail.

2.3. The government as an actor in the urban system

The role of the government in the urban development process differs from that of households and industries in Western Europe inasmuch as the government is supposed to behave in the general interest rather than in its own. As in the case of the other actors the government's objective is an increase of welfare, but it is the welfare of the collectivity it governs that it has at heart. Moreover, the government is the only actor bound by law to maintain and increase certain essential welfare components, such as housing, schools, hospitals, cultural provisions, roads, and other infrastructure, regional industrialization, etc. By so doing, the government influences the level of welfare components in every single region and thus influences people's well-being as well as industries' profitability. Given our assumptions about the behaviour of the other actors, the government, through its actions, can affect that behaviour directly or indirectly, and in this way can direct the spatial development of urban structure. But the government cannot do so to advantage, unless it has a clear view of the future spatial structure it is striving to realize and of the means by which it intends to do so. Whether that condition is always fulfilled, whether indeed it can be fulfilled at all, is an open question. Not only are future developments uncertain, too little is yet understood of the complex relationships between all the elements involved, relationships that in the end determine the outcome of a process set in motion. Until we know how all the elements of the urban system affect, and react to, one another it is impossible to foretell where present developments will lead and what the effect of separate measures on the future spatial structure will be. Under the circumstances, predicting the future becomes a precarious occupation, and trying to direct developments a very hazardous task.

The alternative is for the government to try and base its policy on the preferences held by society, by first trying to determine the effects of each decision on the most important welfare components and on the spatial structure in which these components will function. The desirability of certain developments in the future cannot be appreciated other than in the light of present experience of success and failure. The utmost that can be done is to check the extent to which a measure taken now is going to reinforce positive or negative development tendencies, every sector of spatial development being considered in relation to every other sector.

Spatial development is by nature a very interdependent process, and its planning must consist essentially in *coordinating* the many partial measures that in some way affect the whole. The first step towards coordination is to assess the spatial consequences of each welfare-promoting measure: where is a certain welfare component located, how does it influence the location of other components, and what interaction will result? Similar questions have to be asked with respect to the government's regional and urban policy.

Through its policy, the government tries to promote the well-being of groups in society as well as that of regions. Its *objective function* must therefore express the weighting of both individual and regional interests, extra weights being given, in accordance with the government's political preference, to certain groups in regions that are lagging behind in welfare progress or whose position is deteriorating as the development process goes on. With optimum overall welfare as its objective, the government will try to reduce to a minimum the interpersonal and interregional differences in well-being, or at any rate to provide for a certain minimum level of well-being for all groups and regions under its care.

To achieve its objective, it is not essential for the government to achieve for everybody everywhere exactly the same combination of welfare components. Because a certain trade-off between welfare components is possible, various combinations represent the same level of welfare; the government will endeavour to influence relevant potentials in such a way that for every group and in every region a certain desired level of well-being is attained. How much a certain combination is appreciated depends on, respectively, the preferences of the group or the regional population.

On the assumption that the government has an annual budget at its disposal for the expansion of potentials, i.e. for new housing projects, for creating or stimulating employment, for providing public facilities, and for carrying out infrastructure measures, the government will be confronted with a double choice:

(a) how to allocate government money to the individual regions, those with a relatively low welfare level getting priority;
(b) how to allocate the money functionally within such region to the various welfare components, priority to be given to the components that contribute most to well-being.

The choice becomes even more complicated when a distinction between social groups is made; in that case the government will also have to decide which groups are to benefit in particular from welfare-policy measures.

The regional and functional allocations will finally be affected according to the government's priorities, as embodied in its *social welfare function*. In this function, the total welfare of all regions as well as the various welfare components within each region will be weighted by factors related to the actual regional situation. An increase in welfare in a backward region contributes more to the national welfare than an increase in a prosperous region, and should have priority. Similarly the raising of a relatively low potential within a region is clearly to be preferred to the boosting of a potential that is already on a relatively high level.

Potentials can be raised by the government by means of additional outlays for:

(a) increasing the physical size of a provision while maintaining its quality;
(b) improving the quality of a provision while maintaining its size;
(c) increasing or improving the transport infrastructure.

We must emphasize that the potential of a region for a certain welfare element is improved by public expenditure on that element not only within that region itself, but also in all other (relevant) regions, for a potential, according to the definition given earlier, is the weighted sum of a region's access to that element, whether present in the region itself or in other regions. Interregional interdependence is, in fact, an essential feature of the potential approach. But potentials can be interdependent among themselves as well. Measures directed towards employment will have consequences for both the housing and the amenities potential. Sometimes the influence is direct—e.g. when a new industrial factory ousts a recreation ground—but in most cases the spill-over is the indirect result of effects on transport and traffic. An additional increase in traffic may make provisions less accessible; the construction of a new road, on the contrary, may make them more so.

It is the public authorities' responsibility to distribute public money wisely, taking into account the various interdependences. They may first approach their task in a static way, asking: given a certain situation, and disregarding future developments, what is the best allocation? But reality, as we have seen, is highly dynamic. Every change in regional welfare relationships leads to changes in the spatial behaviour of people and industries, changes that in turn affect welfare relationships. Governmental welfare measures change welfare relationships and so will provoke reactions from other actors. It is also the government's responsibility, then, to take such dynamic effects into account, and if possible, to utilize them consciously as a spatial instrument by which to ensure the welfare of groups and regions even in the long run.

The foregoing argument is elaborated in the Mathematical Appendix.

3

Stages of Urban Development

The conclusion to be drawn from Chapter 2 is that the urban system is subject to a complicated dynamic process, which, if left alone, does not lead to a state of equilibrium, but will always be fraught with friction and produce conflicting reactions from individual population groups. In what follows an attempt will be made to arrange the many spatial changes in the urban system along a few main lines.

To that end, use will be made of an assumed connection between the changes in the structure of the urban system on the one hand and the development stage of a region or town on the other. We assume that each stage is characterized by certain specific urban developments, which tend to be found everywhere unless the government or other actors consciously try to steer developments in another direction, one country's experience probably influencing policy in another. It must be noted that this relationship can vary between countries because the process of accelerated urbanization started at different points in time.

The definition of the successive development stages must perforce remain general. It is based on socio-economic development, its major characteristics being the changes in the structure of the economy and of income level. As far as economic structure is concerned, three very broad stages are conceived: first, the transition from a largely agrarian to an industrial society, second, the transition from an industrial economy to a tertiary economy, and third, the growth of the tertiary sector to maturity. In what follows these three stages will be distinguished, and the spatial changes of a town which can be considered typical of each stage will be investigated. Very broad definitions are envisaged, which will help to schematize to some extent the process of urban change.

As has been said earlier, a description of spatial change must indicate how the behaviour of the various actors in the urbanization process—

households, industries, and governments—in pursuing an increase of welfare causes the urban system to evolve. In this chapter the consequences of the locational behaviour of industries and households will be the main topic. The part played by the government will be less explicitly dealt with, being kept for discussion in Part III.

3.1. The first stage: urbanization

During the first of the three stages distinguished, when a country or region can grow no further as an agricultural economy and gradually becomes an industrial country, the chain of events is fairly obvious. As a result of population growth and the limited possibilities of extending available agricultural land, rural districts will have a growing redundant labour force, entailing a corresponding decrease in income level. When new industrial employment is created, a migration flow will be initiated from the country to the towns where it is concentrated. Because in the early days of the process the income level and the number of hours to be worked daily do not permit a person to live too far from his work, that flow will lead to strong urban concentrations and to a decrease in the rural population. The newcomers are obliged to live in the town itself, in new residential quarters built around the existing centre, near the factories. This first phase is characterized, therefore, by the fast expansion of towns with massive, concentrated town quarters. Similarly, new towns spring up in places that appear favourable to industrialization.

Such a process of urbanization was a characteristic development of all the countries of Europe following the Industrial Revolution in England. In most of them it began in the nineteenth century, but in some, only after the Second World War. We will come to some specific differences between these two groups of countries later.

The phenomenon of accelerating urbanization can manifest itself in different ways. If the country-to-town movement in a country is oriented largely towards one particular town which embodies all modern development, that town has a chance of growing into the national metropolis. However, the movement may just as well orient itself to a number of smaller towns scattered across the country. Whether one or the other development occurs depends not so much on the urbanization process itself as on the historical situation in the country involved, the degree of political centralization or decentralization, and the propensities of a region, or town within a region, for industrialization. Those propensities in turn depend on the town's location in the national and international context, the physical circumstances, the facilities for the supply of raw materials and the dispatch of final products, and on factors of a more political nature such as the policy pursued by the government with regard to industrialization and providing facilities for the establishment of industries and the expansion of towns. Together such factors constitute the conditions and limitations relevant to the locational behaviour of industries as described earlier. Most urban development at this stage is linked to existing urban centres, which until then have functioned as administrative, cultural, religious, commercial, or military centres.

This supports the hypothesis that an existing urban nucleus, with its attendant agglomeration advantages, is highly conducive to successful industrialization, and that its diversification is important for further growth prospects. Yet, in places where the presence of raw materials, a favourable labour market, or good transport prospects compensate for the lack of an existing urban milieu, entirely new industrial towns may come into being.

As far as the spatial structure of a town is concerned, the most important feature at this stage of the urban process is the concentration of the development. Towns go through a phase of concentrated growth amid a stagnant surrounding territory. If there are several urban centres near enough to one another, there is a chance of their growing together to form one agglomeration.

The spatial form of a town is determined to a great extent by the transport facilities and traffic provisions available. The stage of economic development and income level force those who work in the town to go on living there, their choice of residence being limited by available transport provisions. As transport technologies develop, the spatial shape of the town evolves. In the early days of the Industrial Revolution workers had to walk to work, so that houses had of necessity to be built near to factories. With the advent of railways and tramways longer distances could be bridged, and towns expanded along the tracks and around the stations. As public transport in town is the main mode of conveyance, the townsman's mobility is restricted to the town where he lives, which consequently is characterized by a high residential density. Within the town all sorts of public amenities have to be provided for the fast-growing population, in the fields of medical care, hygiene, education, and recreation. As a rule, the creation of amenities follows the growth of employment and of the attracted population after a considerable timelag. Without denying that great social abuse occurs, we conclude that many people increase their well-being in this period by moving from country to town. It is not difficult to appreciate that the highest priority is given to having a job and hence being sure of one's livelihood, however meagre, and that the house and its surroundings are considered less important, as also is the availability of public amenities. It is at the next stage that increase of welfare will be looked for in the elements that are still lacking.

Although this pattern is roughly applicable to both Eastern and Western European countries, it seems worth while to point out some specific features of developments resulting from timelags in Eastern European countries as compared to those of Western European nations.

"In the course of the nineteenth century, Eastern Europe was on the fringe of areas then becoming urbanized as a result of the industrial revolution."[1] The waves of innovation that originated in England—the main growth pole at that time—reached Eastern Europe late and with considerably less impetus. This impetus was largely cushioned by the specific political conditions in the semi-feudal system then prevailing in Eastern Europe.

A gradual increase in the division of labour and the developments in technology created conditions for the emergence of industrial towns. They mainly grew up close to raw-material resources and in areas that formerly had well-developed crafts.

The forms of urban settlement continue to include the following:

—big industrial cities with high spatial concentration of socio-economic activities and of population;
—big and medium-sized conurbations, primarily involved in the extraction of mineral and power-generating raw materials; this form is also characteristically dense and, in its first phase, has a relatively poor pattern of links;
—medium-sized and small towns that function as trading intermediaries for agriculture.

In each of these forms, the levels of welfare in the various town quarters inhabited by different population groups differ considerably. There are no urban transport systems or other urban systems that service the town over its entire territory. Because of the lack of adequate transport services, housing developments are located near town centres and near industrial plants.

Over the period under discussion the big cities and conurbations undergo changes generated mainly by the development of urban transport systems, by the extension of water supplies and sewage systems, the increase in housing construction and the first attempts at town planning. Town-centres become less densely populated, towns continue to expand in space, and new industrial centres and housing developments begin to appear along railway lines for instance. In a few cases, too, new towns are built according to urban layouts and are provided with the basic system of technical infrastructure in their centres. The essentially positive changes in the group of towns under discussion show only one side of the picture; it

---

[1] From S. Herman and J. Regulski, *op. cit.*

must also be pointed out that in all of them slum areas are expanding, as a result of the immigration of untrained rural people.

The third of the above-mentioned forms—the small and the medium-sized towns—were stagnating, at the expense of both living conditions and technical infrastructure.

The retarded and relatively weak impact of the urbanization and industrialization processes in Eastern Europe produced virtually no changes in social or economic relations in the rural areas. The big landed estates, applying traditional methods, were a barrier to progress in agriculture. Accordingly, the already considerable disparity in welfare between village and town worsened in all aspects, becoming one of the most essential factors affecting the processes of urbanization over many decades to come.

Redundant labour in the most densely populated rural areas was growing. Only some of the jobless could find work in towns, as the industries there were still underdeveloped. Moreover, the immigrants lacked the requisite occupational training. This produced a great wave of emigration of the East European rural population to the most advanced West European countries and to the United States.

The nation states that emerged as new or in a new form as a result of the First World War faced huge problems. The necessity of integrating their territories according to new boundaries was the first of these problems. It was often necessary to redesign entire railway networks. Then individual railway lines were combined in a nationwide network. In contrast to the railway, the road system was generally of poor quality. Horses used as draft animals still provided the basic means of transport, as motoring was still in the future.

Some steps were undertaken to prepare the economic integration of these countries; primarily this involved the industrialization of what had earlier been fully agrarian regions. Hence the incentive given to the allocation of new industries outside the existing industrial centres. Regional power-generating systems were created.

Attempts were made to reform the anachronistic agricultural system in order to encourage agriculture output and to help combat rural unemployment. But the manner in which this was undertaken was limited in scope and rather ineffectual.

Governments had to intervene in the towns, where they tried to combat poor housing conditions and the inevitable building speculation by passing laws protecting occupants on the one hand and encouraging housing construction on the other. It was at this time also that the first housing projects on a condominium basis were launched by various social organizations with a view to creating decent living conditions for the less-well-off population groups.

The establishment of appropriate economic bases for the municipal self-governments that were incapable of coping with the new problems presented another serious difficulty. Through subsidies, credit, and concessions granted to private enterprises many towns managed to develop their transport system, their communications, and power supplies. Water and sewage systems and sewage treatment plants, however, did not meet the towns' real needs. No attempts were made to modernize town centres. Many towns were in an economic predicament.

In Eastern Europe the end of the Second World War marked the turning-point. The political system underwent basic changes, at a time when countries were trying to recover from the damages of the war and, in some cases, adapting to changes in state boundaries. Top priority was given to industrial growth.

The industrialization programmes created a huge demand for manpower in the urbanized areas, and this in turn caused powerful waves of migration from the rural areas to the towns. The years of fastest urban growth for the Eastern European countries was between 1960 and 1975.

The migration waves were not caused by economic considerations alone. The continuing disparity in welfare level between town and village was another factor. Towns offered access to education, training, and cultural facilities, with all their inherent advantages. Moreover, farm work, although sometimes well paid, enjoyed little prestige. Gradually emigration to towns resulted in a manpower deficit in agriculture, although this only really became acute in the next period. Another factor conducive to the shift of manpower from agriculture was the development of manufacturing industries, centres of technical services to agriculture, and basic services in rural areas, all of which provided non-agricultural jobs.

But, as previously mentioned, capital shortages during the period of reconstruction and the emphasis on the priority of industrial over other investment naturally reduced expenditures on social infrastructure, which at that time was still considered non-productive. This affected urban development in an important way. If urbanization is measured by the number of people living in towns and by the degree to which towns are equipped with municipal services, then industrialization can be said to have outpaced urbanization during this period.

3.2. The second stage: suburbanization

The second stage is referred to as one of the further developments of the industrial era. Speaking in broad, schematic terms one might say that urban development, after a period when factories spring up everywhere there is a fast accelerating evolution in the economic structure in which towns grow at the cost of rural areas, has now entered a stage of consolidation, with its own characteristic changes in the urban structure. Although towns continue to grow and to attract people from outside, the emphasis at this stage is on qualitative improvement. In terms of the objective functions of the actors as postulated in Chapter 2, it could be stated that—with work available and increasing—priority shifts to better housing and public amenities. These become available as a result of an increase in income, which individually and collectively is spent according to new preferences.

The evolution of motorized transport is a decisive factor in the spatial changes of the town. Extended public-transport facilities and the introduction of buses and private cars which reach areas not connected with the network of trains and tramways widen the scope of residential location. New spacious residential quarters in more pleasant surroundings, "garden towns" sometimes, can now be added to the city. Town parks and green belts are designed; museums, theatres, schools, and hospitals are built in other empty places. In the city centre itself space is reserved for new employment in the tertiary sector, or existing monumental buildings are given a new function as office buildings.

Factories are moved as much as possible to the town's periphery where they are less of a nuisance and yet, thanks to the new modes of transport, accessible. In the town, banks, offices, and the whole complex of administrative and personal services inherent in a complicated, industrial society are accommodated. It is in this period, too, that people begin to live out of town while working in the city. The movement is started by small well-to-do groups who, in terms of time, income, and transport facilities, can afford to move out, and it develops into an inverse migration flow fast growing in volume. To the people involved, living in a quiet rural environment is important enough to outweigh the sacrifice of the money and time required for bridging the distance to their work and the provisions of the town. Given their objective function, they have again increased their welfare, provided that the infrastructure between their new residence and the town is adequate. In very nearly all cases it is the government that is responsible for that infrastructure, thus the government has a powerful instrument with which to influence the spatial pattern of urbanization. Through the construction of infrastructure and the provision of certain forms of transport the government can reinforce or check certain spatial tendencies. The better the transport system, the more a town can expand.

It seems worth while to point out at this stage other features that are more or less typical in Eastern European countries.

In these countries everything connected with production was given top priority. For this reason, and also because of the lack of capital, housing and services were developed at slower rates.

Programmes for urban development were subordinated to plans for industrial growth. With the exception of the big cities, expenditure on the construction of new houses was treated as investment accompanying the construction of new industrial plants. Thus the small and medium-sized towns were left to stagnate, if no industrial plant happened to be located in them. The small towns were particularly affected, as they lost their function as intermediaries between agricultural production and the consumer market after centralized integrated systems of agriculture production and consumption had been created. In contrast to this, regions that formerly had some industry were developed very rapidly to form urban agglomerations. New towns emerged, while those in which new industrial establishments were localized recorded very high rates of growth.

On a parallel with this, ran a strong tendency to increase the size of industrial establishment and to group plants in industrial complexes. The policy underlying this was an attempt to lower prime cost through generalized economies of scale. Big complexes of industry with work forces of up to several thousand people were being established. The location decision for each of these industrial groupings had a powerful effect on the further course of urbanization and spatial structure of the country.

Some of the new plants were localized in less developed regions to ensure their growth. The discovery of new mineral resources also had a strong effect on location decisions. Very often such locations were chosen in order to absorb the redundant labour force from the rural areas around it and to prevent emigration to towns. This again helped to reduce the demand for new dwellings in the towns.

Most plants, however, were localized in the existing large industrial centres. One important aspect of their location was the need for qualified people from rural areas to take jobs in industry.

In contrast to Western Europe, a great number of people were able, as a result of transport services, to go on living in their villages and to travel daily to their place of work in the towns. This kind of commuting increased to such an extent that a special group of workers-peasants emerged, one in which the head of the family had a job in the town while the remaining members of the family worked on small farms. The size of the population group grew in proportion to the implementation of the industrialization programme, which provided for the location of new industrial plants in the less advanced regions.

The vast number of commuters created an immense demand for more extensive mass travel facilities, a sector which was then given top priority. Urban and suburban transport systems were developed (tramways, bus lines, electric trains). Business enterprises built their own independent transport systems for their workers. Private motoring was still insignificant and, at this stage, not supported by the government.

Travel to work, interindustrial relationships between complexes of economic activities and the urbanization of rural areas around the cities and major towns—all these contributed to the development of the cities into so-called urban agglomerations.

The term urban agglomeration denotes a group of settlement units whose aggregate population, economic potentials and functions are distinctly different both in quantity and quality from the other elements of the nation's settlements system. An agglomeration consists of the following spatially and functionally integrated elements:

1. A city or a group of towns which form the central area (the core) of the agglomeration.

2. Smaller towns and urban settlements around the core.

3. Villages whose characteristics have been transformed to the extent that it seems justified to designate them as urbanized areas.

4. Agrarian areas, forests and recreation areas which fulfil service functions for the benefit of the agglomeration's population.

The criteria for delimiting the agglomerations usually depend on the purpose of the given study and on the information available.

Over the period under investigation urban agglomerations grew rapidly in all the socialist countries of Europe. This was the result of the rising rate of economic growth and the concomitant dynamic processes of spatial concentration and deconcentration and of spatial and functional integration. In a number of cases, commuting played a significant role too; this was due to the insufficient housing resources in the central areas of the agglomerations and the concentrated allocation of new industrial workplaces.

In the urban agglomerations, with big towns or cities at their centres, the biggest population and economic potentials were concentrated. The incipient agglomerations emerging in areas of newly discovered raw materials showed the highest growth rates.

The spatial forms assumed by urban agglomerations at this stage were typical of the premotoring stage: starlike patterns along the lines of mass transport.[2]

Generally it can be said that this phase of suburbanization in Eastern Europe became established when social criteria began to gain importance.

At this stage urbanization process involves the development of the social infrastructure to include indispensable elements in the equipment of the urban area. Their importance became widely recognized.

Material production and social infrastructure are mutually interdependent elements in the development process. The development of social infrastructure stimulates the development of material production. Conversely, if the development of infrastructure fails to keep pace with rising social need the development rate of material production may fall, thus adding to the economic and spatial disproportions rather than improving them. An awareness of this situation led to a gradual increase in the allocation of more capital for housing construction and living space and the raising of minimal living standards. Attempts were made to introduce new, more attractive and more diversified architectonic forms to avoid the monotony of prefabricated buildings. A full programme aimed at providing the urban population with a range of services by developing the system of basic services and supplementing it with better facilities in town-quarter centres and town centres began to be put into operation.

At about the same time the working week is being reduced. The extra free time together with the rapid development of private motoring considerably increases spatial mobility which resulted also in increased recreation and tourism. Demands for areas suitable for weekend recreation around the towns is rising. Weekend cottages are being built in increasing numbers.

The increased expenditure for these purposes made possible a decrease in the disparity in welfare level between urban and rural areas. Housing settlements built according to urban standards were provided for the employees of big state-owned farms. The service systems catering for the entire population, both rural and urban, are being extended.

The social policy carried out in rural areas must be seen as one element of the overall policy for the development of agriculture. Nutrition had become one of the most fundamental problems. The rising rate of consumption tends to exceed the increase in agricultural output, since in the previous period less capital was invested in agriculture than in industry. Hence every country has to undertake a comprehensive programme for increasing its agricultural output.

Another result of high industrial investment was that in towns manpower deficits become more and more acute. Given the shortage of labour, increasing employment no longer furthers economic growth. An increase in labour productivity becomes the priority.

These conditions lead to the introduction of programmes for what was called intensive industrial development. Programmes for rapid technological advance are carried out. Attention is focused therefore on selected industries, in accordance with the desired distribution of labour.

---

[2] S. Herman and J. Regulski, *op. cit.*

The modernization of industry involves the scrapping of obsolete factories. Small industrial plants disappear too. Production is concentrated in separate industrial quarters. Although this has a number of advantages, it does increase commuting distances, a circumstance women find particularly troublesome. Once this was realized, small industrial establishments were reintroduced in residential town quarters.

The development of a network of services, the rising rate of housing construction, the specific features of industrial development, the reshaping of the layout of road networks to suit the development of motoring—all these factors contribute to the transformation of the internal structure of towns. At the same time, continuing urban development reinforces the structure of urban agglomerations and even leads to the emergence of urbanized regions or districts where several agglomerations coalesce. In some cases, such regions extend beyond state boundaries. Their spatial form also tends to change. Whereas formerly agglomerations developed generally along main transport lines, at present the areas between those zones tend to fill in, as private motoring increases individual mobility. Thus agglomerations tend to change in shape from a starlike pattern to that of a "fat blot" spilling out in all directions.

These big concentrations of population, industry, and services necessitate the development of complicated systems of technical infrastructure. Heating systems for towns and agglomerations must be constructed as also regional water supplies and sewage systems. The growing intensification of internal links within agglomerations leads to the adjustment of the road network to take the increasing traffic flow and also to tie in with the development of regional transport systems. The number of commuter journeys does not alter, but people travel for a different reason. Whereas formerly people travelled to work because of the housing shortage in towns, now they are more likely to travel because they choose to live away from the centre. More and more people prefer to live on the outer fringes of agglomerations. Town centres become less populated whereas the suburbs witness rapid, occasionally uncontrolled building activity.

The development and intensification of primarily industrial production damages the environment in a variety of ways. Accordingly, plans for the protection of natural amenities on national, regional, and agglomeration scale have been worked out. In some areas industrial development has been reduced, to the benefit of the tourism and agriculture on which the economic development of those areas depends.

The stage which urban development has now reached makes it imperative for plans to be coordinated. Hence the increasing significance of spatial plans. In Eastern Europe as in Western Europe, long-term plans for the countries' space-economic development and for comprehensive regional development have been worked out. Those plans are gaining in importance.

It is necessary to improve upon previous methods of planning to take into consideration new phenomena and fast changing circumstances. Correct planning of the development of agglomerations is especially important.

The stage of development discussed in this chapter is characteristic of a number of cities of relatively recent vintage, while the socialist countries of Eastern Europe seem still to be in the early phase of this stage.[3]

The last phase of this stage, particularly in Western Europe, is notable for the tremendous increase in the use of the private car and the heavily increased demand for the elements of social infrastructure which in due course come within almost everybody's reach. The positive and negative consequences of the introduction of the private car in urban spatial structure can hardly be overestimated. The possession of a private car makes it easier for distances to be bridged regardless of the location of a public

---

[3] S. Herman and J. Regulski, *op. cit.*

transport network. Commuter travel is affected in particular: people no longer need to live near their work or near public transport services. For large categories of society an entirely new situation is created; they can now live anywhere within a given wide area and still have adequate access to all the elements they consider important to their welfare. A job in town can easily be combined with living a considerable distance away, and a number of central provisions in the city will remain within reach. The tendency that first manifested itself in the building of garden cities is now being continued on a vast scale.

It is typical of all European countries where cars are common that many· people aspire to a house of their own in green surroundings outside the town. The policy of governments and housing authorities rarely resists that tendency; on the contrary, they stimulate the outward movement by encouraging large-scale construction outside towns, hence the massive suburbanization that marks the present spatial changes in many European towns. The population now grows in the suburbs of central towns, while in the cities themselves the number of inhabitants is often decreasing.

Now that towns are spreading over an ever-increasing area, the terms "urban area" or "urban district" have become more accurate than "town". Central city and suburban surroundings are functionally united, and within the larger area homes and places of work are spatially distributed, as are other places for recreation, which also have space requirements in the same area.

3.3. The third stage: desurbanization and inter-urban decentralization

The development described in Section 3.2 may be called positive in that it meets prevailing needs as regards housing, recreation, medical care, shopping, etc., and makes for greater living comfort and has done away with overcrowded town quarters. But there are also obvious negative consequences, and it must be feared that they will get worse as the scale of suburbanization becomes larger, the worst problems being those relating to traffic.

For agglomerations which find themselves in this stage of urban development, existing road infrastructure can no longer cope with the thousands of commuters who on weekdays try to get into town and find a parking space. The resulting congestion makes all kinds of workplaces and central provisions in the city centre less and less accessible. Attempts are being made to improve the centre's accessibility by improving the infrastructure and stimulating the use of public transport.

To improve the infrastructure, it is necessary to clear areas for new access roads, to modify the layout of streets, and to provide extensive parking facilities. The required space is found mostly in the old residential quarters, which date from the time when urbanization first started; they are sacrificed in order to modernize and reconstruct the centre. People living there find themselves compelled to seek refuge on the outskirts or joining those who have moved to suburban municipalities.

When the measures to increase the centre's accessibility by car prove ineffective, there is a good chance that new service industries will decide to settle in the city centre. Of course, increased traffic intensity will once more lead to congestion, and to additional nuisance for the townspeople, thus giving them an additional stimulus to move to the suburbs. Indeed, it will grow increasingly difficult, and require ever higher investments, to improve the situation.

Measures that aim at transferring an increasing proportion of the traffic in city centres from private cars to public transport have the same indirect result. Improvement of the public transport services and their extension to the suburban municipalities around the town does indeed make for easier access to the town by the suburbanites, but at the same time makes people even more willing to leave the town for the suburbs. The tendency towards progressive suburbanization and the attendant continuous need to adapt and extend the infrastructure and the public transport system at even higher cost will be maintained for as long as tertiary industries find it worth while to be located in the town centre. As it functions on an increasingly large scale, the tertiary sector needs more and more space, which has to be claimed from the older living quarters in the town. Wherever the process described here occurs, the decline in the number of inhabitants of the central town may be seen to continue.

In the end, this development threatens the prosperous existence of the town itself. When the inhabitants leave town, provisions such as shops, schools, and medical care will soon follow. If the city centre remains congested there comes a time when offices, too, are attracted to a location in the suburbs, or even outside the urban district in other parts of the country, which so far have escaped full urbanization and remain more accessible because there is no congestion. Not only towns but suburbs also will decline in population, while elsewhere still rural areas will be transformed into urban areas, often at the cost of the natural environment and valuable farmland. This is the stage of desurbanization, attended by inter-urban decentralization; we shall discuss it in more detail later on.

In Table 3.1 and in Figs 3.1 and 3.2 the different stages of urban development are shown. During the first stage the central city (or core) is growing fast, and the suburban (in this case still rural) ring around the central city

TABLE 3.1.
Stages of development in a Functional Urban Region (FUR)

Stage of development[a]	Classification type	Population change characteristics			
		Core	Ring	FUR[b]	
I Urbanization	1 Absolute centralization	+ +	–	+	} Total growth
	2 Relative centralization	+ +	+	+ + +	
II Suburbanization	3 Relative decentralization	+	+ +	+ + +	
	4 Absolute decentralization	–	+ +	+	
III Desurbanization	5 Absolute decentralization	– –	+	–	} Total decline
	6 Relative decentralization	– –	–	– –	
IV Reurbanization	7 Relative centralization	–	– –	– –	
	8 Absolute centralization	+	– –	–	

[a] The terms urbanization, suburbanization, desurbanization, and reurbanization are here defined in the following manner: Urbanization is in force when the growth of the core dominates that of the ring, while the FUR as a whole is growing. Suburbanization is in force, when the growth of the ring dominates that of the core, while the FUR is still growing. Desurbanization takes place when the decline of the core population leads to a decline of the population of the whole FUR. Reurbanization takes place when the share of the core population in the total population of the FUR is increasing again, in type 7 because the core declines slower than the ring, and in type 8 because the core is growing again while the ring is still declining.

[b] The concept of Functional Urban Regions is discussed fully in Chapter 5.

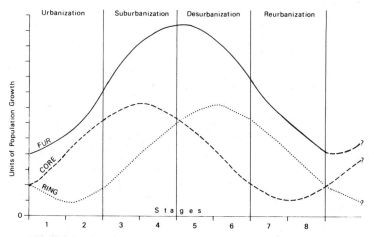

Fig. 3.1. Population size of the core, ring, and functional urban region (FUR) in different stages of urban development.

declines or remains constant in population. This is the stage of urbanization. In the second stage (suburbanization) the growth of the central city starts to slacken while gradually the population of the suburban ring increases. The proportion of the population living in the ring increases considerably. In the third stage, that of desurbanization, the point has been reached where the population of the central city starts declining to such an extent that it results in an absolute decline of the population of the whole Functional Urban Region (FUR).[4]

The spatial development of this stage in the urban life cycle is very different from that in the previous stage; no longer is the process characterized by incremental contiguous or tree-ring-like growth. The absolute decline of the central city and its suburban commuting hinterland is associated with a rapid increase in the population and jobs in and around the large (dominant) FUR within 50–120-kilometre range where the small and medium (subdominant or satellite) urban areas are to be found. The satellite cities will usually be at an earlier stage in the urban life cycle than the dominant FUR (Fig. 3.3), this being reflected, among other things, in their smaller size. The rate of inter-urban decentralization will be more rapid the greater the regional dynamism.

The people who are tempted to migrate to the small and medium-sized cities may well be returning from a suburban to an urban life-style, albeit in a smaller-sized urban centre. Such a move may reflect a wish to avail themselves of several benefits: better access to work, improved service

---

[4] For definition of Functional Urban Regions, see Chapter 5.

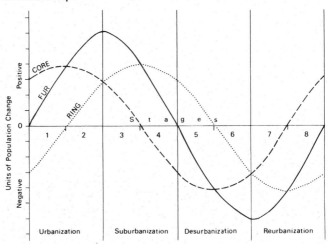

Fig. 3.2. Population growth and decline of the core, ring, and functional urban region (FUR) in different stages of urban development.

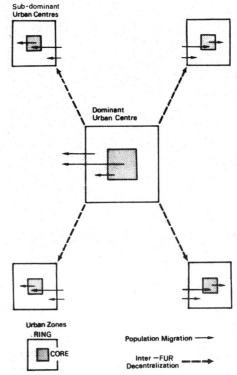

Fig. 3.3. Stage of desurbanization: out-migration from the dominant centre and inter-urban decentralization.

provision and more open space, often more living space, access to the countryside and a wide range of recreational opportunities, and the wish to avoid the numerous economic and social costs incurred in the original location.

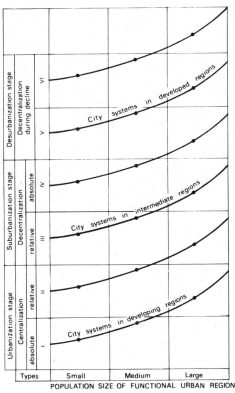

Fig. 3.4. Population centralization and decentralization related to city size and the level of regional economic development.

The decentralization of the population and latterly of jobs is a process that characterizes urban systems in the desurbanization stage, irrespective of their size, region, or location in relation to other cities; what varies is the *rate* at which this process operates (Fig. 3.4). Cities in the prosperous regions of a country are apt to decentralize more rapidly than those in the peripheral or less prosperous regions. The size of the city system is also important in explaining rates of decentralization, mostly because size is related to the density of the urban core, which is linked in turn to the stage that a city has reached in its life cycle. The process is also determined by the role that a FUR performs in the national settlement system.

3.3.1. *The national settlement system*

The development of inter-urban decentralization of large FURs in the desurbanization stage and the rapid expansion of medium-sized towns is one aspect of city-system interdependency in advanced economies. Individual FURs no longer grow and change in isolation but are greatly influenced by events taking place elsewhere in the national settlement system. The interdependencies are affected by flows of goods, services, information, decisions and capital between various sectors of the economy. As most employment is concentrated in urban areas, the pattern and intensity of such flows will inevitably determine the processes of urban development.

The properties of city-systems have traditionally been described in terms of rank-size distributions, central place theory, growth pole theory, hierarchical diffusion, and the like. It is questionable whether such inductive rules and theories are at all useful in explaining the contemporary spatial organization of settlements. An understanding of these processes will ultimately depend on improving knowledge on the perception, evaluation, and decision-making of major actors who in turn are largely influenced by the structural components of the social means of production.

3.4. The future: reurbanization?

The process of accelerated desurbanization and deconcentration described above depicts one alternative future. Another is that of reurbanization (Fig. 3.1). In Western Europe, both local and central governments have woken up to the possibility of turning the tide in their large cities and restoring their image, by rehabilitating the existing housing stock, introducing urban-renewal programmes, improving the traffic situation, creating pedestrian zones, and upgrading the social infrastructure. Whether such measures will persuade more people to stay in the city and also entice people from outside the city to come and settle is hard to say. The trend towards the desurbanization in the largest cities seems too general and so strong that only through the application of a most rigorous policy could significant results be expected, and such a policy has yet to be developed. It seems inevitable, then, that in the not too distant future our cities, and in particular the large FURS, will be facing a host of problems. The rather pessimistic considerations contained in subsection 3.4.1 may be helpful in explaining what these problems are.

3.4.1. *Stages of desurbanization*

It was concluded in Section 3.4 that the developments taking place in the large FURS of Western Europe are likely to continue, and the question arises as to what evolutionary stage we may expect next. We shall try to identify and systematize these stages.

Let us start with the simple definition that the total area of urban land in use for urban purposes in a FUR equals the product of the number of households (population divided by the average growth of a household) and the average land-use per household. So:

$$A = \frac{P}{f} s \qquad (3.1)$$

in which

A = total area of urban land,
P = total population,
f = average household size,
s = area per household.

We may also write (3.1) as:

$$\dot{A} = \dot{P} + \dot{s} - \dot{f}. \qquad (3.2)$$

The point over the symbols indicates that we are dealing with relative changes over a period of time.

Now we do know one or two things about the quantities contained in the right-hand side of equation (3.2). The total population of a FUR has been mentioned more than once in previous pages, and we know that there comes a point where the population of large FURS falls into a decline, and $\dot{P}$, thus, becomes negative.

$\dot{s}$ is the relative growth of area per household. We assume that it will remain positive, but decreasingly so. In other words, we assume that the demand for land per household will grow further (land for provisions and job opportunities included), but to a decreasing extent.

$\dot{f}$, lastly, representing the relative growth of the average household, is negative. The average household is becoming even smaller. The scope for reduction being, naturally, limited—a household can hardly consist of less than one person—the relative decrease will tend asymptotically towards zero.

The four factors have been combined and are shown in Fig. 3.5.

During the first period $(0 - t_A)$ the population, the number of households, and the total demand for land all increase. Desurbanization, though heralded by the evolution through time of the various quantities, has not yet set in. t_A is the crucial point in time where the first stage of desurbanization $(t_A - t_B)$ begins, the stage at which the population falls but the number of households as well as the total demand for land for urban purposes goes on rising. At t_B the loss in population exceeds the consequences of decreasing family size; the number of households begins to fall in the absolute sense. It is the second stage of desurbanization, in which the phenomena of decline are becoming more manifest. The last point of interest is t_C, beyond which neither the greater demand for land per household nor the smaller average size of households can compensate any longer for the loss of population, so that the absolute demand for urban land is diminishing, too. Beyond point t_C the town faces the necessity of contracting in the absolute physical sense.

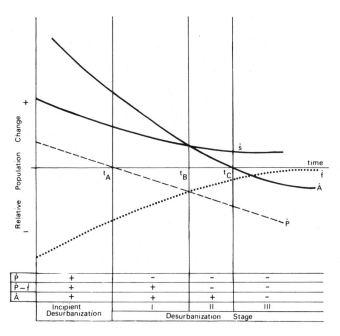

Fig. 3.5. Stages of desurbanization: the sequential decline of population, the number of households, and the total demand for urban land.

One wonders what the consequences of such an evolution may be. Some people may believe that the processes of expansion and contraction are bound to occur side by side and will continue to do so. So, if the urban population at a given moment shows a marked predilection for smaller agglomerations and medium-sized towns, that is—according to these people—a natural phenomenon, not to be considered unusual, and to be accepted with all its consequences.

Now, to form an opinion on this matter we need to look at the phenomena a little closer and to evaluate them. In this way we can decide whether it is preferable to let the process run its course, check it, or try to reverse it.

3.4.2. *The consequences of desurbanization*

To find out what the consequences of desurbanization are, let us look at each stage somewhat closer. It will soon appear that the consequences are cumulative, that is to say, new results add themselves to, and reinforce, earlier ones. The whole process has a snowball effect and threatens to lead eventually to a town's total downfall, turning a living entity into a ghost town.

The first stage is marked by continuing physical expansion of the town (land area, houses) and simultaneous contraction of the population. Though there are no exact figures available, from the little evidence there is it may be inferred that the change in the net migration—a major cause of population loss—can be imputed partly to the increased exodus of the higher income groups and partly to the dwindling desire among the same kind of people to migrate from rural areas to a big city. Even if the average income of the remaining group of city dwellers continues to rise, the increase in the number of well-to-do inhabitants may well entail a cutback in the total income of the urban population. And what that means is obvious: less turnover for retailers, for the catering trade, and for other services. Public transport, already facing fast-growing deficits, sees its market dwindle, while the municipality finds its budget has shrunk and its social services are financially undermined.

It is quite likely that housebuilding will stagnate as soon as the second stage is felt to be imminent. By the end of the first stage there will be no net demand for new houses; after it, there will be a surplus. This would not be so bad in a period of fast rising incomes, when houses tend to become obsolete quickly because of the dwindling demand for cheap houses; in such a period it would be feasible to build new houses and discard the cheaper and older ones. But in a state of desurbanization one cannot count on fast income growth, any more than on the need to replace the existing housing stock at a high rate with new ones more in line with higher incomes. The less so, when there is an increasing tendency to renovate existing houses instead of simultaneously demolishing old and constructing new houses.

What is certain is that the more the demand still existing for new houses is met at this stage, the greater will be the surplus in the next stage. That is why it is highly opportune to investigate carefully during the first stage— which a series of towns have already entered—the extent to which we are justified in meeting the demand for housing in view of the absolute decline in total demand for houses that can be envisaged in the foreseeable future.

The second stage, as has been said before, is marked by a shrinking population, a decrease in the number of households (hence less demand for houses), but a continuing increase in the use of urban land. A drop in the demand for houses causes great difficulties in the construction trade, the more so because incomes can hardly be expected to rise in the period involved (see above). In fact, it is now the turn of employment in the building sector, alongside that in the service sectors, to plummet. In stage 2 more houses will be demolished than built, the cleared sites being used for other purposes, for the total demand for land is still increasing at this stage.

Awkward questions will now present themselves. If houses have to be demolished at all, which shall we condemn, those recently renovated, or the newer ones of lower quality? Where shall we start demolishing, in the central town or in the ring? Is it likely, or not, that more land will be required exactly where the housing stock is becoming smaller? Such questions are difficult and far from encouraging. The picture is becoming grim.

The climax, or rather the nadir, of the transformation is reached in the third and last stage, in which to the former disintegrating processes is added the phenomenon of cleared sites being left unused. In this period there is neither reason nor money left to give those sites a meaningful purpose. The most logical solution is perhaps to raze the worst quarters to the ground and to turn them into green belts, so that eventually there will be a green-bordered town core surrounded by an urbanized, but shrinking ring of built-up areas. It seems logical, but would it be wise? Much capital is being invested in the renovation of precisely those old quarters, capital that is bound to depreciate faster than its investors envisage.

The alternative, starting the demolition programme in the ring, is not attractive either. By so doing, too much capital would be sacrificed to adapt the town to the diminishing number of households. Advantage would be gained from clearing bits of land which could for the greater part be restored to its original agrarian function (it would be better not to dwell on the cost price of those bits of land, however).

Wherever one starts the town is going to fall to pieces, showing gaps where land lies fallow. There will be a general decline which cannot fail to affect social relationships, crime, and cultural decay. Cultural and social bloom in the midst of absolute economic downfall is not a regular feature of our society.

The prospects are no less than frightening. All the more so if the process of economic decline has to be paid for with vast loss of capital in all sectors of economic life. Large-scale urban decline, in the sense of an overall deterioration of urban functions, could have serious consequences for society in the countries afflicted, for it heralds the complete ruin of the urban culture of the twentieth century. If such a disastrous state of affairs is to be warded off, reurbanization must be brought about fast and resolutely. Traffic problems dominate the present urban scene, and to resist urban decline it will be necessary first of all to solve them. Experience has taught that the desired effect can be expected only from measures that manage to reduce traffic demand. Such measures must restrain suburbanization, and accomplish the reurbanization of central towns by giving new support to their residential function. To that end, industries will have to be redistributed across the whole urban area in such a way that home-to-work distances are reduced and the use of the existing infrastructure made less one-way than it is now. Positive measures to achieve these ends have already been introduced in several European countries.

It has been assumed that shifts in the economic structure, the level of well-being, and the government's policy underlie the described spatial changes in urbanization. The changes involved are seen primarily as the results of actions by individuals and industries, motivated by their aspirations to a higher welfare level. The government's role in the process has been discussed far less explicitly. Yet, as representative of the general interest the government has a very specific task. When the urbanization process is perceived to lead to discrepancies and unacceptable loss of well-being for certain groups of the population—the result, at least partially, of past government action—it is for the government to regulate and adjust matters in such a way as to ensure more welfare for everybody. In the section dealing with urban actors attention has already been given to the role of the government in general and to its objectives and powers of action.

In Part III the theory of urban policy and its instruments will be treated more specifically. Actual urban policy, within the context of regional policy, will also be treated after the empirical analysis of urban development trends in Part II.

PART II

Empirical Analysis of Urban Development Trends

4
Introduction

4.1. Objectives

The statistical analysis of urban development in fourteen European countries presented in Chapters 6 and 7 meets the following objectives:

(i) to provide a European view of settlement-system changes in the period 1950–1975, a time when significant shifts in spatial structures occurred in many countries;
(ii) to develop a better understanding of the processes that currently guide the pattern of urban growth, stagnation, and decline;
(iii) to provide a (partial) test, at national and cross-national levels, of the general theory of urban development which has been outlined in Chapters 2 and 3, with special emphasis on the link between the spatial development of urban systems and changes in the level of economic activity and the production structure.

4.2. Concepts, methods, and definitions

Few would dispute that the main feature of European urbanization is its *diversity*: diversity of origin, dispersal concentration, and degree of urbanization. To try to capture European urbanization as one overall concept would therefore be a very dubious undertaking. For example, rates of decentralization are critically affected by the residential density in the old part of the cities and in new quarters or suburbs as well as by the income distribution in the centre; while the extent to which central residential functions and small-scale industrial employment remain also plays an important part. Houses and small industries are still a feature of many large central European cities, and while they persist will always depress their rate of decentralization.

The notion of decentralization itself needs some explanation. Quite different processes may underlie a decentralizing trend, such as people

49

moving out of the centre of the city, a tendency towards smaller families, or the—purely administrative—measures of annexing small towns and villages.

Their very diversity can make European cities good subjects for empirical analysis, by permitting the evaluation of a full range of development hypotheses; on the other hand, this same diversity can make the analysis a hazardous enterprise. The relevant methodologies must be chosen with great care.

4.2.1. *Problems in cross-national comparative research*

The analysis of urban change within a single country poses many methodological problems and among the most difficult are:

(i)   The comparability of data from different censuses;
(ii) the homogeneity of definitions of urban areas and whether the definitions are "fixed" or "floating";
(iii) the choice of appropriate urban zones to illustrate certain development processes;
(iv) the choice of the years and dates of observations;
(v)   the assessment of the effect of boundary changes and of reorganization of administrative areas.

These problems highlight the need for comparable data and for ways of defining urban areas, as well as for standardized data, spatial units, and time series at the *national* level.

A comparison *between* countries is additionally hampered by:

(i)   the lack of synchronization between national censuses;
(ii) the lack of standardized data among national censuses;
(iii) the fact that the available data do not relate to standardized spatial units. This makes it virtually impossible to compare small areas; in measuring urban change and population movements appropriate geographical units are indispensable;
(iv) the fact that, because of differences in national statistical systems, some variables, such as commuting and employment structure, are available for a limited number of countries only.

To achieve the objectives of this study and to try to overcome the limitations imposed by the differences in national data units, the empirical analysis is based on two quite different types of spatial units, of which one corresponds to the concept of *Functional Urban Regions* and the other that of *Urban Municipalities*, distinguished by their functional location within the urban system (city cores, ring, or unclassified places).

The data sets do not permit an analysis of urban development stretching over a long period. This is a serious limitation when hypotheses concerning the evolution of city *systems* are to be tested. Because many variables are available for one period only (1960–1970), we have to rely mainly on cross-section analysis. However, from the evidence offered by such a diverse group as the fourteen European countries involved in this project, it is possible to infer much about the processes underlying urban development. A time-series analysis of the development of total population and net migration during three periods (1950–1960–1970–1975) complements, moreover, the analysis of functional urban regions.

TABLE 4.1.
Summary of the CURB Urban Information System

Spatial frame characteristics	Analysis of functional urban regions	Analysis of urban municipalities
Number of regions/places	189	4375
Variables	Area	Area
	Population[a]	Population
	Natural change[a]	Natural change
	Migration[a]	Migration
	Employment	Employment
	Employment structure	Employment structure
	Commuting	Commuting
Dates[b]	1960, 1970	1960, 1970

[a] Also available for 1950, 1975.
[b] For France: 1954–1962–1968–1975.
   For Bulgaria: 1965–1975.

Too narrow a view would, of course, result from equating urban change with urban-population change. Growth and change can take many forms. Towns can increase in size (simple growth), or change their internal organization (demographic change), and relationships may change in consequence. They may grow economically (manifest in the income of their inhabitants) or spatially (in area, extent, or intensity). All these different types of growth can be measured in several ways; inevitably, however, population is the one variable of which statistics are generally available, and our analysis relies heavily on it. Other indicators, such as employment and employment structure, are used whenever possible, but mostly at the expense of a smaller sample. Variables, dates, and sample sizes in the FUR and Municipality analyses are summarized in Table 4.1.

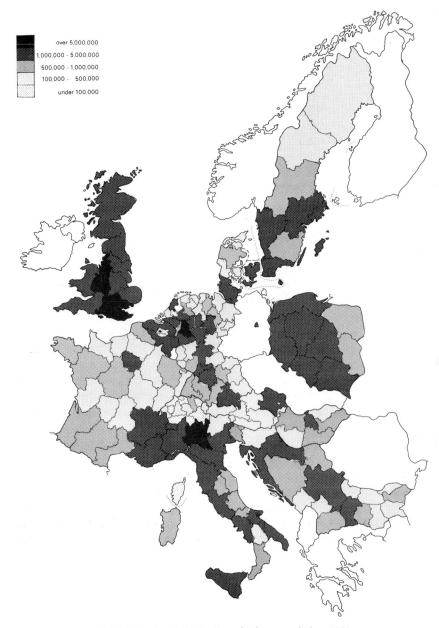

Fig. 4.1. Regional distribution of urban population, 1970.

4.2.2. Samples of urban municipalities

One part of the empirical analysis of urban change in Europe is based on a sample of some 4375 urban places distributed among fourteen countries of Eastern and Western Europe. (See Fig. 4.1.) The sample is composed of places with populations of more than 10,000 inhabitants in 1970. A place cannot be called "urban" on the strength of its population size alone. Its character is derived from other variables, among them its population density and its function within the agglomeration. For this reason data on the area and function of the urban places in our sample were also collected.

On the other hand, a minimum size was considered necessary for a place to be defined as urban, and it was felt that by setting a threshold of 10,000 inhabitants most of the truly urban places within the participant countries could be captured. Table 4.2 reproduces the main characteristics of the urban municipality sample. It should be pointed out that quite a few of the urban places analysed are not agglomeration centres, but are part of agglomeration rings. Although such places do not exercise central functions, they are unmistakably urban in character. Indeed, an analysis of urban change should not only be concerned with separate urban centres or places, but also with whole agglomerations. These can be composed of urban places and localities with less than 10,000 inhabitants. The latter aspect is taken care of in Chapter 5 describing the empirical analysis of the FURs.

A cross-national comparison of urban change based on the sample of urban municipalities is hampered by lack of homogeneity in the systems which are compared. Single urban places differ in area and in how they are distributed in relation to population size. The former difference in particular seems to have no direct connection with a theory which tries to explain urban change within a national urban system in relation to development of the national economy. Both the area of a town and the distribution of its population should rather be considered as an outcome of many years of historical progress and institutional arrangements, going back to topographical as well as political origins. Indeed it appears from figures and percentages in Table 4.2 that the urban system within the national system of settlements is far more important in some countries than in others, and that the hierarchies of urban places also vary very much between countries.

TABLE 4.2.

National population totals and the proportion resident in the FUR and UM samples, 1970

Country	Total resident population		Population resident in functional urban regions FUR sample		Population resident in urban places with more than 10,000 inhabitants UM sample		Population resident in places with less than 10,000 inhabitants	
	Absolute	%	Absolute	%	Absolute	%	Absolute	%
W. Germany	60,650,599	100.0	29,092,946	48.0	36,653,759	60.4	23,996,840	39.6
Great Britain[a]	53,978,538	100.0	32,656,116	60.5	50,780,196	94.1	3,198,342	5.9
Italy	53,744,737	100.0	13,554,275	25.2	34,956,460	65.0	18,788,277	35.0
France	49,778,540	100.0	15,913,793	32.0	16,048,545	32.2	33,729,995	67.8
Poland	32,642,270	100.0	12,151,100	37.2	14,904,216	45.7	17,738,054	54.3
Yugoslavia	20,522,972	100.0	2,657,511	12.9	6,258,370	30.5	14,264,602	69.5
Netherlands	13,045,785	100.0	4,441,970	34.1	10,495,425	80.4	2,550,360	19.6
Hungary	10,322,099	100.0	3,589,504	34.8	5,450,307	52.8	4,871,792	47.2
Belgium	9,650,944	100.0	2,630,450	27.3	5,348,292	55.4	4,302,652	44.6
Bulgaria	8,728,000	100.0	3,056,210	37.1	4,370,460	50.1	3,357,540	49.9
Sweden	8,076,903	100.0	2,792,763	34.6	7,502,979	92.9	573,924	7.1
Austria	7,456,403	100.0	3,484,002	46.7	3,268,698	43.8	4,187,705	56.2
Switzerland	6,269,783	100.0	2,199,064	35.1	2,842,849	45.3	3,426,934	54.7
Denmark	4,937,579	100.0	2,187,909	44.3	3,865,811	78.3	1,071,768	21.7
Total for 14 European countries	339,805,152	100.0	130,486,735	38.4	202,746,367	59.7	137,058,785	40.3

[a] Consisting of England, Wales and Scotland.

5

The Sample of Functional Urban Regions

The growing interest in the identification of functional regions around urban areas reflects the feeling that political and administrative boundaries no longer provide a meaningful spatial framework for the analysis of urban activity systems. The concept of Functional Urban Regions is in practice interpreted as referring to nodal regions, identifying urban centres, and delimiting zones dependent on those centres. For lack of data on the interaction between small areas, functional urban regions are in fact delimited solely by the size of journey-to-work flows. It is essentially a spatial-interaction approach, trip distribution being considered a fundamental determinant of urban spatial structure.

The concept may be theoretically sound, but the search for consistent definition of areas persists; admittedly, the areal units to define cores and rings, and the boundaries traced with the help of percentage commuting cut-offs, represent but arbitrary thresholds, and the FURs may not therefore be strictly comparable, even within one national system at a given point of time, and even with delineation criteria remaining the same through time.

The FUR concept developed above was applied to the urban systems of fourteen European countries with the following results.

(a) All urban regions organized around central cities with populations of over 200,000 people in 1970 were regarded as FURs.

(b) Because a city's regional function within the national urban hierarchy may be more important than its absolute size, so that not-so-large towns in some systems may be functionally comparable with larger ones in others, some regions around *regional* centres of less than 200,000 inhabitants were also counted as FURs.

TABLE 5.1.
Functional Urban Regions by country

Country		FUR	Population 1975[a]	Country		FUR	Population 1975[a]
Austria (7)	1	Vienna	2053.4	**FRG** (cont.)	20	Kiel	362.1
	2	Linz	369.1		21	Bielefeld	345.6
	3	Graz	353.8		22	Lübeck	284.7
	4	Salzburg	275.1		23	Münster	268.1
	5	Innsbruck	237.4		24	Osnabrück	256.1
	6	Klagenfurt	160.8		25	Freiburg	229.3
	7	Bregenz	99.4		26	Ulm-Neu Ulm	226.9
					27	Bremerhaven-Nord	227.1
Belgium (5)	1	Brussels	1050.7		28	Würzburg	207.1
	2	Antwerpen	662.3				
	3	Liège	432.5	**GB** (43)	1	London	8534.2
	4	Ghent	218.5		2	Birmingham	2841.9
	5	Charleroi	208.6		3	Manchester	2066.2
					4	Glasgow	1605.7
Bulgaria (8)	1	Sofia	1205.8		5	Liverpool	1430.7
	2	Plovdiv	539.0		6	Leeds	1206.9
	3	Varna	329.0		7	Newcastle	1034.6
	4	Russe	258.5		8	Sheffield	954.8
	5	Pleven	235.6		9	Coventry	754.1
	6	Burgas	219.9		10	Bristol	726.4
	7	Stara Zagora	153.6		11	Edinburgh	658.3
	8	Vratza	105.2		12	Nottingham	639.5
					13	Leicester	550.5
Denmark (5)	1	København	1454.8		14	Stoke	527.9
	2	Aarhus	316.6		15	Portsmouth	540.3
	3	Odense	227.7		16	Teesside	485.4
	4	Aalborg	210.0		17	Cardiff	473.4
	5	Esbjerg	81.4		18	Southampton	462.6
					19	Hull	425.7
France (22)	1	Paris	8424.0		20	Oxford	367.1
	2	Lyon	1152.8		21	Brighton	355.9
	3	Marseille	1004.5		22	Bournemouth	343.6
	4	Lille	928.5		23	Derby	334.6

5	Bordeaux	591.4
6	Toulouse	495.2
7	Nantes	433.2
8	Nice	437.5
9	Rouen	389.4
10	Strasbourg	355.2
11	St Etienne	334.5
12	Nancy	278.6
13	Le Havre	263.9
14	Clermont-Ferrand	224.7
15	Rennes	213.2
16	Montpellier	204.9
17	Orléans	204.5
18	Dijon	203.1
19	Caen	182.6
20	Limoges	164.7
21	Amiens	152.5
22	Besançon	124.0

	24	Reading	325.5
	25	Luton	336.5
	26	Plymouth	326.4
	27	Norwich	283.2
	28	Southend	279.1
	29	Sunderland	260.9
	30	Motherwell	286.2
	31	Bolton	265.1
	32	Slough	263.1
	33	Chatham	253.8
	34	Doncaster	249.3
	35	Swansea	247.6
	36	Blackpool	235.7
	37	Wigan	234.5
	38	Aberdeen	231.7
	39	Ipswich	229.8
	40	Cambridge	225.7
	41	Preston	207.0
	42	Dundee	201.7
	43	Huddersfield	200.3

FRG (28)

1	Rhein-Ruhr	9454.4
2	Berlin	2122.1
3	Hamburg	2269.9
4	München	1787.8
5	Frankfurt-Offenbach	1713.3
6	Stuttgart	1704.6
7	Hannover	914.4
8	Mannheim-Ludwigshafen	891.5
9	Nürnberg-Furth	885.3
10	Bremen-Delmenhorst	864.2
11	Wiesbaden-Mainz	715.3
12	Karlsruhe	477.9
13	Bonn-Siegburg	477.3
14	Aachen	467.6
15	Augsburg	406.3
16	Rheydt-Mönchen-Gladbach	393.6
17	Saarbrücken-Völklingen	383.4
18	Kassel	377.4
19	Braunschweig-W'f	372.0

Hungary (6)

1	Budapest	2499.6
2	Miskolc	363.4
3	Debrecen	302.7
4	Szeged	243.1
5	Győr	234.7
6	Pécs	216.4

Italy (18)

1	Roma	3698.9
2	Milano	2676.2
3	Napoli	n.a.
4	Torino	1699.9
5	Genova	830.9
6	Palermo	747.4
7	Firenze	632.5
8	Bologna	615.7
9	Catania	539.3
10	Bari	526.4

(continued overleaf)

Table 5.1 (*cont.*)

Country	FUR		Population 1975[a]	Country	FUR		Population 1975[a]
Italy (*cont.*)	11	Venezia	469.4	Poland (*cont.*)	14	Bydgoszcz	328.0
	12	Verona	434.5		15	Lublin	310.3
	13	Brescia	403.9		16	Radom	203.8
	14	Padova	397.7		17	Bialystok	190.2
	15	Cagliari	333.9		18	Torun	157.8
	16	Messina	300.0				
	17	Taranto	297.3	Sweden	1	Stockholm	1493.5
	18	Trieste	296.6	(7)	2	Göteborg	568.1
					3	Malmö	243.5
Netherlands	1	Rotterdam	1115.3		4	Uppsala	138.1
(7)	2	Amsterdam	1092.4		5	Norrköping	119.1
	3	The Hague	730.1		6	Västerås	117.9
	4	Utrecht	422.1		7	Linköping	109.2
	5	Eindhoven	442.3				
	6	Enschede	329.3	Switzerland	1	Zürich	714.4
	7	Groningen	266.1	(7)	2	Basel	375.2
					3	Genève	323.2
Poland	1	Katowice	3392.7		4	Berne	235.8
(18)	2	Warszawa	2113.3		5	Lausanne	229.7
	3	Lodz	959.3		6	Lucerne	156.8
	4	Krakow	885.6		7	Winterthur	108.2
	5	Gdańsk	775.5				
	6	Bielsko-Biala	623.7	Yugoslavia	1	Belgrad	925.6
	7	Poznan	579.5	(8)	2	Zagreb	593.7
	8	Wrocław	568.9		3	Skopje	342.0
	9	Kielce	410.8		4	Sarajevo	252.2
	10	Walbrzych	404.0		5	Ljubljana	207.9
	11	Szczecin	390.9		6	Novi Sad	182.8
	12	Opole	373.3		7	Pristina	90.0
	13	Częstochowa	344.3		8	Titograd	63.3

Total number of FURs: 189.   [a] In thousands.   n.a. = not available.

TABLE 5.2.
Distribution of total FUR population by size class, 1960

Size class in millions	Number	Total population 1970 (in thousands)	% of total population
>5	3	25,900	21.53
2–5	9	20,300	16.87
1–2	15	20,400	16.96
$\frac{1}{2}$–1	27	19,100	15.88
$\frac{1}{4}$–$\frac{1}{2}$	62	21,100	18.12
<$\frac{1}{4}$	73	12,800	10.64
Total	189	120,000	100.00

(c) In a FUR all contiguous and surrounding municipalities having a commuting rate of over 15 per cent to the central city were included; failing commuting data, other interaction variables were used or official agglomeration definitions accepted.

The total number of FURs thus defined was 189; their names, grouped by country, and their 1975 populations are presented in Table 5.1.

In the 189 FURs presented in Table 5.1 there live over 115 million people, approximately 31 per cent of the total population of the fourteen countries analysed.

TABLE 5.3.
National distribution of FURs by size class in 1975

Country	Number of FURs	Size class					
		>5 m	2–5 m	1–2 m	$\frac{1}{2}$–1 m	$\frac{1}{4}$–$\frac{1}{2}$ m	<$\frac{1}{4}$ m
GB	43	1	2	4	8	25	3
FRG	28	1	2	3	5	16	1
France	22	1	0	2	2	8	9
Italy	18	0	3	1	6	8	0
Poland	18	0	2	0	6	7	3
Bulgaria	8	0	0	1	1	3	3
Austria	7	0	1	0	0	4	2
Netherlands	7	0	0	2	1	4	0
Sweden	7	0	0	1	1	1	4
Switzerland	7	0	0	0	1	4	2
Hungary	6	0	1	0	0	5	0
Yugoslavia	8	0	0	0	2	2	4
Belgium	5	0	0	1	1	1	2
Denmark	5	0	0	1	0	2	2
Total	189	3	11	16	34	90	35

TABLE 5.4.
Degree of primacy of largest FUR in each country

Country	Primate FUR	% of total population in primate FUR
Denmark	Copenhagen	29.67
Austria	Vienna	27.63
Hungary	Budapest	22.63
Sweden	Stockholm	18.29
France	Paris	16.46
GB	London	15.92
FRG	Rhine-Ruhr	15.58
Bulgaria	Sofia	13.80
Switzerland	Zürich	11.47
Belgium	Brussels	11.09
Poland	Katowice	9.56
Netherlands	Rotterdam	8.75
Italy	Rome	5.18
Yugoslavia	Belgrade	4.51

It is a well-known empirical fact that any urban system shows a regular distribution pattern of cities, with a small proportion of large cities, a greater one of medium-sized towns, and numerous small townships. So it is not surprising to find in Table 5.2 just that distribution in our sample, which represents the sum of national distributions, the number of FURs in each class being inversely related to the size of the towns in it. Out of the total 189, some twenty-seven FURs are mammoth cities, three of them housing over 5 million people. While representing only 14 per cent of the total number of FURs in the sample, they account for over 55 per cent of their total population. The 135 FURs with populations under half a million account for no more than 28 per cent of the total FUR population.

The number of FURs in each country tends to vary with the size of the national population as well as the level of urbanization; Table 5.3 gives a review.

With the exception of Yugoslavia and Switzerland, all countries have at least one city which has a million or more inhabitants. The larger countries show well-ordered hierarchies of cities; many smaller ones are dominated by their prime city; the capitals of Austria, Denmark, and Hungary, for example, account for 20 to 30 per cent of the total population, as Table 5.4 shows. By contrast, the prime cities of Poland, the Netherlands, Italy, and Yugoslavia accommodate less than 10 per cent of the countries' total population.

6

Trends of Urban Development: Urban Municipalities, 1960–1970

To make the sample of urban places, census data for population and employment were collected for the years 1960 and 1970, or in the case of some countries, for 1961 and 1971. Data for two of the countries, Bulgaria and France, did not follow the general pattern, and refer to 1965 and 1975 for Bulgaria, and to 1962 and 1968 for France.

Table 6.1 shows the respective population increases in the urban municipalities of each country and in the countries as a whole, as well as the ratio between them.

From a comparison of the percentages of columns (1) and (2) of Table 6.1 it appears that while in the socialist countries there was a strong tendency towards concentration during the sixties, in Austria, Germany, and Switzerland, at the other end of the scale, the urban population grew less rapidly than the national population, perhaps, among other reasons, because the suburbanization in those countries involved places of less than 10,000 inhabitants. In the Netherlands, Great Britain, and Denmark, where a large proportion of the national population is already living in urban places, the two rates of change are equivalent.

6.1. Population change by size group

By the very process of agglomeration, the pace and the sense in which an urban place develops are determined largely by its size. While the large urban centres, the agglomeration cores, tend to show a loss of pace or, even, population, smaller places, particularly those on the fringes of agglomerations, tend to develop very rapidly.

61

TABLE 6.1.
Urban population change in the CURB countries, 1960–1970 (percentages)

Countries	% Increase in the municipalities population (1)	% Change in the national population (2)	Ratio (1)/(2) (3)
Bulgaria (1965–75)	29.6	6.1	4.85
Hungary	14.5	3.6	4.02
Yugoslavia (1961–71)	39.3	10.6	3.70
Poland	20.1	9.6	2.09
Italy (1961–71)	13.6	7.7	1.76
Sweden	9.4	7.7	1.22
Belgium (1961–70)	5.5	5.0	1.10
Denmark	8.2	7.7	1.06
France (1962–68)	7.4	7.0	1.05
Netherlands (1960–71)	13.9	13.8	1.00
GB (1961–71)	5.1	5.3	0.96
Switzerland	13.7	15.5	0.88
Austria (1961–71)	3.4	5.4	0.63
FRG	4.4	12.5	0.35

Table 6.2 compares some features of urbanization in America and Europe during the sixties. The group of urban places of between 250 and 500 thousand inhabitants as well as that of between 10 and 25 thousand inhabitants grew more rapidly in Europe; in the group of 100–250

TABLE 6.2.
Changes in urban places and urban population by size groups, 1960–1970

Size groups (thousands)	Changes in urban population U.S.		Changes in urban population in European countries	
	in 1000	%	in 1000	%
Over 500,000	3166.4	11.1	568.3	1.2
250–500	−299.8	−2.8	1998.8	14.1
100–250	2511.1	22.1	5067.4	20.2
50–100	3567.1	28.5	5053.0	21.0
25–50	3014.2	23.6	6454.0	21.4
10–25	2608.4	17.4	7317.5	20.8
Totals and average rates	14,567.5	16.0	26,450.0	15.0

Source for the US data. These data have been derived from G. V. Fuguitt and C. L. Beale paper: Recent trends in city population growth and distribution, published in *Small Cities in Transition: The Dynamics of Growth and Decline*, ed. by H. J. Bryce, Cambridge, Mass., 1977, pp. 13–28.

thousand the rate of change was more or less the same in both samples; in all other size groups the American growth rates were higher than the European ones.

The same pattern applies to the relative change in urban population. In most size groups change rates for the population of American urban places exceeded those for the inhabitants of European towns; the exceptions were the group between 250 and 500 thousand and the group with less than 25,000 inhabitants.

What development patterns do these percentages show? First of all it can be observed that across all size groups urban change was far more homogeneous in Europe than in the United States. In Europe all groups of urban places with less than 250,000 inhabitants grew at about the same pace, while in the United States their rates of growth differed considerably. The same can be said of the changes in the number of urban places by size groups, at least as far as the groups of places with between 25 and 250 thousand inhabitants are concerned.

In the US urban places of between 25 and 50 thousand inhabitants, i.e. the small cities by American standards, grew fastest.[1] Their rapid growth has continued since 1970, many people leaving the large cities to settle in smaller places, a phenomenon that can also be observed in Western European countries.

Suburbanization is a phenomenon that is common to the US and to all CURB countries, with urban places of more than 250,000 inhabitants changing less than the other size groups; therefore, the share of the largest towns in the total urban population tends to diminish both in the US and in Europe. In the US the share of urban places with more than 250,000 inhabitants dropped from 43.2 per cent in 1960 to 39.9 per cent in 1970; in the fourteen CURB countries together it dropped from 35.0 to 31.7 per cent in the same period.

Some attention will now be given to development in individual countries; relevant data are presented in Table 6.3. It seems that heavily populated municipalities everywhere tend to change less quickly than places with fewer inhabitants; however, within the individual size groups there are considerable differences between countries. In most West European CURB countries negative growth can be observed over the relevant period in the largest cities (those counting between 250 and 500 thousand and those of over 500,000), whereas in the East European countries and in Italy the largest urban centres developed very rapidly. As a general observation the homogeneous growth pattern characterizing the size groups of under

---

[1] See Herrington J. Bryce, editor, *Small Cities in Transition: The Dynamics of Growth and Decline*, Cambridge, Mass., 1977, in particular the introduction with the statement of the problem.

TABLE 6.3.
Change in urban population by size groups in the CURB countries, 1960–1970
(in thousands)

Countries	10–25	25–50	50–100	100–250	250–500	More than 500
Austria (1961–71)	18.6	17.6	7.4	8.5		−0.8
Belgium (1961–70)	20.7	7.8	37.8	0.9	−1.2	5.1
Bulgaria (1965–75)	40.3	−1.2	48.2	−16.1		20.5
Denmark	4.0	11.6	94.1	10.3		−13.7
FRG	73.3	14.5	14.2	7.8	14.4	−4.5
France (1962–68)	6.6	12.9	13.1	14.7	36.2	−2.4
GB (1961–71)	2.6	15.5	33.4	8.8	5.0	−12.5
Hungary	13.2	11.6	4.4	82.9		12.2
Italy (1961–71)	7.5	28.3	−2.4	65.2	17.7	13.4
Netherlands (1960–71)	27.1	25.4	17.3	10.0	9.2	−7.4
Poland	17.9	53.6	26.9	17.0	6.0	37.0
Sweden	−2.7	15.7	−8.8	80.1	11.9	−7.7
Switzerland	63.4	46.5	8.6	2.0	−4.0	
Yugoslavia (1961–71)	10.8	68.1	65.5	49.5	−27.3	124.2

250,000—as pointed out in the comment on the total sample of municipalities—results from very divergent national tendencies. In some countries (Belgium, Bulgaria, Denmark, Great Britain, the Netherlands, Poland, and Yugoslavia) the flow to smaller towns had already started. As the sample includes countries in an advanced stage of urbanization as well as countries in a preliminary stage, it appears that the tendency for small towns to grow very rapidly is not inherent to one particular stage of urban development, but can manifest itself in various stages.

As far as the smallest size group is concerned, some countries—Switzerland, the Federal Republic of Germany—show remarkably high rates of population change against others—Sweden, Denmark—where the rates are very low indeed.

In summary, comparison of urban change by size groups in Europe and the United States has shown that while the aggregate European trends are similar to those observed in the US, there are significant differences, particularly in the rates of change by size groups, between individual countries. For the largest towns the rate of change seems inversely related to the level of economic development reached in the countries involved.

6.2. The regional distribution of urban change

In Section 6.1 it was suggested that the population development of urban places is related not only to size but also to location. More precisely, it can be shown that the rate of change is affected by the level of economic

TABLE 6.4.
Regions with the fastest and slowest rates of urban population change, 1960–1970

Country	Fastest growing region		Slowest growing region	
	Name	Rate	Name	Rate
Yugoslavia	Macedonia	59.7	Voyvodina	19.0
Bulgaria	North-east M.	39.8	South-west[a]	21.6
Poland	Central-East	39.3	Central[a]	15.6
Switzerland	Sierre-Sion	30.8	Zürich[a]	9.0
Belgium	Brabant-Walloon	28.4	Walloon Reg.	−0.3
Netherlands	Drenthe	26.2	North Holland[a]	8.7
Italy	Latium (Rome)[a]	25.8	Umbria	2.0
Hungary	North. Transdanubia	24.6	North. Lowland	7.0
FRG	München	20.4	Süd Württemberg	−14.0
France	Languedoc	19.2	Rég. Parisienne[a]	−5.0
Austria	Salzburg	17.6	Wien[a]	−0.1
Sweden	Stockholm[a]	17.1	Middl. Norrland	−4.9
GB	East Anglia	14.1	Scotland	1.0
Denmark	South Jutland	11.8	Zealand[a]	7.0

[a] Regions where the largest town of the country lies.

development, which varies not only among countries but also among regions. It is interesting, therefore, to collect information about urbanization patterns on the regional level. A rough idea of the influence of economic factors on urban development can be gathered by analysing the regions where it was fastest or slowest, as is done for all fourteen countries in Table 6.4. The regions with the highest growth rates appear to belong to one of three categories:

1. regions in which either the capital or the largest city of the country (Stockholm, Latium) is located;
2. regions bordering on the principal metropolitan area (Brabant-Walloon, East Anglia);
3. regions that have just started to develop (Macedonia, Sierre-Sion, Drenthe, Northern Transdanubia, Languedoc, Salzburg, South Jutland).

In the first category, rapid growth can be attributed to the process of concentration; in the second, to progressive suburbanization; the regions of the third category often owe their development to a regional policy aimed at supporting economic growth in selected regions. Switzerland shows an interesting pattern of its own: its decentralized urban development seems to be an effect of the labour shortages prevailing in traditional, economic centres on the location policy of entrepreneurs.

The relatively bad performance of low-growth regions seems to spring mainly from the development of their principal urban place. In seven out of

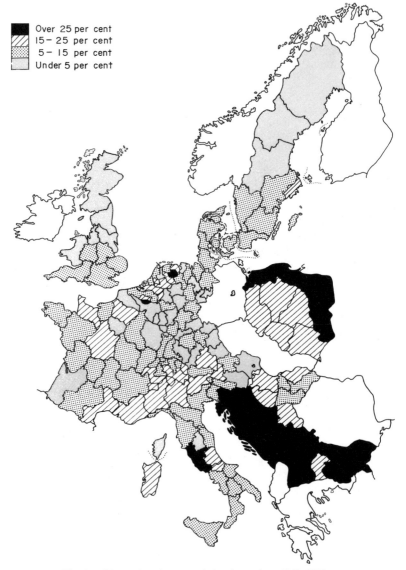

Fig. 6.1. Change in urban population by region, 1960–1970.

fourteen cases (marked by ") the lowest growth rate is scored by regions containing the country's largest town; the remaining seven slow-growing regions have stagnant economies.

In general, regions of fast urban growth are to be found east of the line running from Sardinia to the regions in Western Poland; other rapidly urbanizing regions are to be found on both sides of the Alps, and, in France, along the Atlantic and Mediterranean coasts. Another group of rapidly urbanizing regions is located in the Benelux countries. The urban population in the north of Europe, on the contrary, grew only slowly (see Fig. 6.1).

6.3. Urban change and the functional classification of urban municipalities and regions

In Chapter 3 a model is presented which links the spatial development of an agglomeration to the development stages of the economy. In such a model the development of an agglomeration is supposed to divide into a concentration phase and decentralization phase. Concentration is supposed to occur in the early stages of economic development, when the core of an urban agglomeration grows rapidly. Later on, the development of economic activities sets a suburbanization process in motion, marked by the rapid growth of urban and non-urban places belonging to the ring around the core city. To test the validity of the theory, the performance of urban places at different positions within agglomerations was verified; Table 6.5 presents some of the results. In one case (that of Italy) separate analyses were carried out for the whole of Italy (I), for the northern regions includ-

TABLE 6.5.
Urban population change according to functional areas, 1960–1970

Countries	Change in core urban places (%)	Change in the ring urban places (%)	Change in the unclassified urban places (%)
Austria	2.7	12.8	4.7
Belgium	n.a.	n.a.	n.a.
Bulgaria	30.1	21.0	21.4
Denmark	n.a.	n.a.	n.a.
France	n.a.	n.a.	n.a.
FRG	n.a.	n.a.	n.a.
GB	−0.9	15.5	−4.8
Hungary	18.3	11.8	1.2
Italy (I)	13.5	27.4	7.3
Italy—North (I_1)	11.0	40.7	18.5
Italy—South/Centre (I_2)	16.2	16.1	1.2
Netherlands	7.3	34.0	22.9
Poland	n.a.	n.a.	n.a.
Sweden	n.a.	n.a.	n.a.
Switzerland	5.6	43.0	17.3
Yugoslavia	40.8	37.9	42.7

n.a. = not available.

ing Tuscany (I_1), and for the central and southern regions (I_2) to do justice to the characteristics of the changes in urban population on the regional level, pointed out earlier. The percentages referring to the population growth in the cores and rings are particularly interesting; in the Western European countries the rates are low for the cores and very high for the ring places, which means that in the sixties suburbanization proceeded more rapidly there than in the other countries. The same is true of the northern regions of Italy. In contrast, the other half of Italy and the Eastern European countries show a growth pattern marked by the concentration of people in the cores.

In order to obtain a typology for regions of the urbanization process like the one designed for the analysis of FUR data (see pages 55ff.) the data on the change in urban population by functional areas were regionalized. In Part I, as well as in the FUR analysis, eight development phases, i.e. four concentration and four decentralization phases, may be distinguished. It should be kept in mind that a regional urban system may comprise more than one agglomeration and also contain urban places which have not been classified in these data. For the purpose of the analysis it is assumed, however, that differences in economic development within one region do not markedly affect the regional urban system; the various agglomerations and single urban places in a region are considered parts of one regional urban system, obeying the laws governing the development of this system as a whole.

It should further be noted that all core places of a region are counted as such, but that only communities whose population exceeded 10,000 in 1970 count as ring places. By definition, agglomerations lacking ring cities of more than 10,000 inhabitants were considered to be in the first phase of development. Only for Switzerland was it possible to consider all the ring places, thus obtaining the correct picture.

Table 6.6 is based on the population-change data for the decade 1960–1970, classified according to the function of the individual urban places.

It appears possible to arrange the separate regional urban systems in the various development phases in an order which corresponds to the geographical succession of European countries from East to West; that it is by and large also the order of the levels of economic development will come as no surprise. The subdivision of Italy into a developed North and developing central and southern parts is reflected in the classification of the two groups of regions by urbanization phase. The assumption could have been proved more convincingly if comparable information on the regional economies of the CURB countries had been available, a statistical requirement that is, however, difficult to satisfy.

TABLE 6.6.
Regional urban systems and urban-development phases, 1960–1970[a]

Countries	No. of region urban systems	Urban development phases								No. of urban places
		1	2	3	4	5	6	7	8	
BG	8	2	6							88
H	6	3	2	1						126
YU	8		6	2						148
I	18	2	5	11						876
I₁	8		1	7						432
I₂	10	2	4	4						444
A	7	1	1	4		1				57
CH	13	2	1	8	2					92
NL	11		2	8	1					286
GB	10			3	6	1				1059
Total	99	12	28	48	9	2				3608

[a] For the definition of the phases of urban development, see Part I.

6.4. The demographic components of urban change

It has already been pointed out in Chapter 3 that urban development is marked by phases of demographic concentration and decentralization. It is predictable, therefore, that urban change is largely determined by net migration. To verify that, first of all, the share that net migration had in the population change observed in urban centres of the different size groups in the period 1960–1970 was computed. The percentages found are presented in Table 6.7; to avoid confusion, the percentages referring to population losses have been underlined.

Except in countries like Denmark, the Netherlands, and Italy, where the birth rates were still relatively high, the population change in the different size groups of urban places was dominated by the net-migration component. It can be observed in particular that in countries where concentration predominates, the net-migration component of the growth of urban population tends to increase with the size of the urban place. In countries where decentralizing tendencies are at work, however, the net-migration component tends to diminish as the urban places become larger. Finally we see that net migration is largely negative (though appearing with a positive sign in the table) in the size group registering a population decrease. There seems to be, then, a correlation between the share of net migration in the change of urban population by size groups and the development phase of the national urban system. From a more detailed analysis by region three kinds of regions clearly emerge. There are, first of all, two large city-regions

TABLE 6.7.

Net migration as a proportion of the population change 1960–1970, according to size groups

Country	Population size groups (thousands)								
	10–20	20–30	30–40	40–50	50–100	100–200	200–500	500–1000	Over 1000
Austria	25.5	37.9	12.4	56.6	60.0	71.7	65.1	5.4	−498.2
Belgium	52.1	10.1	−38.8	−22.9	28.3	42.3	65.3	53.8	112.2
Bulgaria	53.9	42.1	53.0	52.8	57.1	55.7	63.9	49.3	
Denmark	10.1	36.0	41.0	−5.5	10.4	−23.6	34.2		
FRG	—	51.1	45.5	48.3	32.9	0.05	273.9	233.5	207.7
France	55.5	48.8	55.3	52.1	58.9	46.8	50.3	49.0	138.3
GB	59.6	60.3	62.4	53.6	36.6	−33.6	575.3	142.9	113.6
Hungary	18.1	63.0	73.5	82.5	76.2	81.8			108.1
Italy	−19.3	15.0	16.9	43.4	33.1	50.5	9.9	−8.8	29.3
Netherlands	24.0	40.4	33.2	−7.1	17.2	−18.6	−16.2	189.6	
Poland	51.6	56.1	56.0	62.2	57.1	57.8	60.5	66.2	
Sweden	6.2	54.9	43.7	60.9	55.8	54.1	45.8	107.7	
Switzerland	55.4	61.8	52.4	35.5	12.6	−40.9	254.9		83.0
Yugoslavia	76.1	65.3	75.4	60.6	70.2	73.4	71.9	70.8	

with a declining population but a positive migration balance: Vienna and Berlin. Probably their net migration is positive, not so much because they should be recuperating after a period of decay, as because the available data refer to an area that is larger than the core areas, by the definition used elsewhere, so that the exceptional position of Vienna and Berlin is, after all, less interesting than it seemed at first sight. The second type of region has a negative net migration combined with either a population increase or a population decrease; they are found either at the periphery of the CURB study area—the northern part of Sweden, the northern part of Great Britain, the southern part of Italy—or among the regions with stagnant industries—the coal and steel regions of northern France, the southern part of Belgium, the western part of the Federal Republic of Germany. The third and largest category comprises the regions that combine positive net migration with an increasing urban population.

With a view to identifying the migration flows within the European urban system it was tried to analyse how the shares of net migration in the change of urban population relate to the size of urban places and to their function in the agglomeration. The relevant data are presented in Table 6.8, which also contains the share of the population change in each size-function group (or cell) in the total change of urban population for the purpose of comparison. Unfortunately, the analysis was confined to the eight countries for which a functional classification of urban places was available. The underlined figures for cores in Great Britain and Switzerland indicate negative net migrations.

The percentages of Table 6.8 point to the concentration of urban growth in cores and ring places; the share of unclassified urban places in the total change in urban population was relatively small, with the exception of those in the Netherlands, which accounted for one-fourth of the total. In general it can be concluded from the table that the change in urban population in the European countries during the analysed period was governed by the development of the agglomerations, and more in particular by that of cores in East Europe, and by that of ring places in West Europe.

It seems worth while to consider the evolution of cores and rings separately.

For the cores two kinds of development can be recognized. In Great Britain, the Netherlands, and Switzerland, the growth of urban population in cores was achieved exclusively by urban places with less than 100,000 inhabitants, larger cores either stagnating or registering population losses. By contrast, in the urban systems of Italy, Austria, Yugoslavia, and Hungary, it was the larger cores, those with more than 100,000 inhabitants, that absorbed between one-third and one-half of the total increase, the smaller cores developing at a slower pace; evidently concentration was still

TABLE 6.8.
Relative urban population change and net migration as a component of urban population change according to size and location of urban area

Country	Size	Core municipalities		Ring municipalities		Unclassified municipalities	
		Urban population change (%)	Net-migration component (%)	Urban population change (%)	Net-migration component (%)	Urban population change (%)	Net-migration component (%)
Hungary	≤ 100,000	38.8	75.6	7.3	53.1	2.0	−89.2
	> 100,000	51.9	97.1	—	—	—	—
Yugoslavia	≤ 100,000	11.8	66.6	51.7	69.9	2.1	78.1
	> 100,000	34.4	98.9	—	—	—	—
Bulgaria	≤ 100,000	47.9	53.0	4.1	49.4	3.7	47.6
	> 100,000	44.3	59.9	—	—	—	—
Italy	≤ 100,000	15.1	38.6	25.6	48.6	14.5	−62.2
	> 100,000	44.8	29.5	—	—	—	—
Austria	≤ 100,000	28.4	35.4	21.9	60.9	12.1	−20.7
	> 100,000	37.6	242.1	—	—	—	—
Switzerland	≤ 100,000	32.7	25.5	65.9	60.5	2.3	35.5
	> 100,000	−0.9	163.9	—	—	—	—
Netherlands	≤ 100,000	34.2	6.0	39.6	47.4	24.3	21.9
	> 100,000	1.9	−1459.8	—	—	—	—
Great Britain	≤ 100,000	21.2	−6.3	128.1	69.3	6.0	71.4
	> 100,000	−62.2	169.1	6.9	68.9	—	—

in progress there. That is also true of Bulgaria, although there the smaller category developed marginally more rapidly than the larger ones.

All ring places, except for a few in Great Britain, have less than 100,000 inhabitants; that makes the analysis of their development trends simpler. In the decentralizing countries (Switzerland, the Netherlands, and Great Britain) the population increase in ring places accounts for at least 40 per cent of the total increase. In all other countries except Yugoslavia the share of ring places in total increase of urban population does not exceed 25 per cent; in Yugoslavia the corresponding share is about half the total, a figure that is to be attributed largely to the functional classification applied in that country. This classification, being based on the principle of "areas of influence", counts very few cores but very large ring areas; some 86 per cent (128 out of 148) of the urban places were defined as ring places.

Now that the proportion of cores and rings in the total increase of population has been considered, we must assess how important the migration component is to urban demographic development; the net migration shares of each functional category of urban places and for both size groups are also given in Table 6.8. Again, it is convenient to make a distinction between the developments of net migration in the cores and rings. As far as the cores are concerned two kinds of behaviour can again be perceived, one in centralizing, the other in decentralizing urban systems. In decentralizing urban systems (Great Britain, the Netherlands, Switzerland) net migration is negative in cores of more than 100,000 inhabitants, and either negative or slightly positive for cores of fewer than 100,000 inhabitants; except in Switzerland there appears to have been no large-scale immigration into medium-sized and small cores. On the other hand, net migration was an important factor for the ring places. The observations could give rise to the hypothesis that people migrated away from large agglomerations and large cores to the rings of medium-sized and small urban cores.

The centralizing urban systems in the sample show very large positive net-migration shares for the larger cores and large net-migration shares for the smaller ones. Here, more than in the decentralizing systems, does the demographic growth of the cores seem to be fed through migration flows.

In the ring places, quite homogeneous behaviour of the net-migration variable prevails, its share in the total increase of population varying from 47.4 per cent in the Netherlands to 79.3 per cent in Great Britain. Except in countries with relatively high natality rates (the Netherlands, Italy, Belgium), net migration contributed most to the population increase of the urban places located in rings. That proves how dynamic are these places, where, as already pointed out, the urban development of the most mature urban systems was largely accomplished. It also constitutes another pointer towards the necessity to analyse urban development on the basis of an agglomeration sample.

6.5. The relation between employment and population change

Another important variable to be considered is employment. In Table 6.9 the average growth rates of population and of employment are presented together with the shifts in the employment structure during the analysed decade. The first observation to be made is that the employment variable has a wider range of growth rates than the population variable: Austria shows a negative rate, while Bulgaria, Yugoslavia, and Poland have growth rates exceeding 40 per cent.

Another interesting point is that where there is rapid growth the tendency is for employment growth rate to lead that of population, while with slow growth the opposite tendency prevails. These tendencies bear out how important a growing demand for labour is for the development of urban places.

For a number of countries some comment can be made on the shifts in employment structure. In six out of the nine countries for which the relevant information is available, the share of industrial employment in total employment was diminishing in the study period; in one other country (Yugoslavia) it did increase, but only slightly. So the growth of our sample

TABLE 6.9.
Total employment change and shifts in the employment structure (1960–1970)

Nations	Urban population change (%)	Total employment change (%)	Shifts in employment structure	
			Industrial (%)	Services (%)
Austria	3.4	−0.53	−5.28	5.77
Belgium	5.5	3.33	−5.81	4.63
Bulgaria	29.1	44.69	n.a.	n.a.
Denmark	8.2	14.38	−2.69	5.23
France	7.4	8.49	n.a.	n.a.
GB	3.1	1.87	n.a.	n.a.
Hungary	14.5	15.15	5.53	−0.33
Italy	13.6	10.48	−0.69	0.88
Netherlands	13.9	15.09	n.a.	n.a.
Poland	20.1	40.87	n.a.	n.a.
Sweden	9.4	8.25	−3.61	10.10
Switzerland	13.7	19.86	−4.42	4.72
Yugoslavia	39.3	40.24	0.99	−3.48

n.a. = not available.

of urban places during the decade analysed went hand in hand, at least on the national level, with a decline in the industrial and a rise in the tertiary share in total employment. It is interesting to note that in the two East European countries for which the relevant statistics are available, tertiary employment showed a downward trend.

6.6. Some conclusions

From the comparison of urban growth rates in Europe and the US it emerged that the greatest differences were recorded for the groups of urban places of over 250,000 and between 50 and 100 thousand inhabitants. While in the US the largest cities, that is to say the cities with over 500,000 inhabitants, grew at a steady pace, in Europe similar cities were demographically stagnant. The opposite applies to towns of between 250 and 500 thousand people; they lost population in the US, but gained quite a lot in Europe. The population of urban places counting between 50 and 100 thousand inhabitants grew faster in the US than in Europe, thus confirming the recently formulated theory that people are moving away from large to medium-sized towns, notably those housing between 50 and 100 thousand people. Quite a few works recently published in the US deal with the resurgence of medium-sized towns. There is no such tendency discernible on the aggregate level of the fourteen countries of our sample. It does appear, and in all size groups up to 100,000 inhabitants, when the urban development within single urban systems is considered. In Europe the rapid growth of the smaller towns may perhaps be regarded as the outcome of both the decentralization process inside agglomerations and the tendency to leave the largest agglomerations for smaller independent urban centres.

The growth of urban centres has a regional and a national dimension. Within a nation there will be some regions where urban growth is rapid and others where the urban population is stagnating or diminishing. In Western Europe, regions with rapid urban growth or regions of urban stagnation in some instances transcend national borders; examples are the Alps region, with rapid urban growth, and the coal-and-steel regions on the borders of France, Belgium, and the Federal Republic of Germany, where the urban population is stagnant.

Ordered according to the typology of urban-development phases presented in previous chapters, individual regional urban systems were found to follow the geographical succession of countries for East to West Europe. This shows that in Western Europe the regional urban systems were in an advanced state of decentralization, while in Eastern Europe they were still in the early stages of concentration.

The pattern of urban development in the regional urban systems, from concentration to decentralization, can only derive from voluminous migration flows. Unfortunately it has not been possible to collect data on the origin and destination of the migrants, and so these remarks rely only on the balance of the migration flows to and from the individual urban places, that is to say on their net migration. In Western European countries the net migration is observed to shrink, and finally to turn negative, with the increased size of the places; in the East European countries, the reverse is true: the larger the place, the larger the net migration. More specifically, in countries where decentralization tendencies are active within agglomerations, the net-migration component is particularly large in places of fewer than 100,000 inhabitants; in countries where concentration tendencies are at work, on the contrary, the share of net migration in the change of urban population is larger for urban places with more than 100,000 inhabitants (which may be defined as cores).

7

Trends in Urban Development: Functional Urban Regions, 1950–1975

The theory of urban development presented in Part I postulates a relation between a country's stage of development and the change in its urban spatial structure. As in Chapter 6, that will be the starting-point for empirical analysis.

The analysis, focused first on the cores and rings of functional urban zones, should verify the theoretically assumed relationship. If it is found to be consistent, it can serve as a basis for classifying cities into groups with similar developmental characteristics.

7.1. Population-growth performance by urban zones

The central city, or urban core, will be the first object of analysis. It is a logical choice, as the concept of functional urban regions rests heavily on nodal structures; moreover, the cores of Europe's cities have for many centuries been the traditional cultural, economic, political, educational, and innovative centres. Centres of cities have been the propelling force for the vitality of nation states, and the hub of urban networks in national settlement systems. The relative growth performance of the population of the urban cores since 1950 will first be considered.

The annual growth rates of the FUR cores (Table 7.1) show a very clear and consistent tendency: irrespective of country, size of total population, or time period, the direction of change is *negative* in all cases. For some countries (Italy, Poland, Hungary, Bulgaria, Yugoslavia, and Austria) the growth rates remain positive, but the rates are declining over time; for some others (Great Britain and Belgium), the growth rates are actually

TABLE 7.1.
Annual growth rates of the FUR cores

| Country | Annual growth rates of FUR cores | | | Direction of change | |
	1950–60	1960–70	1970–75	1960–70 minus 1950–60	1970–75 minus 1960–70
FRG	n.a.	+0.03	n.a.	n.a.	n.a.
Italy[a]	+2.47	+0.98	+0.11	—	—
GB	−0.02	−0.55	−0.92	—	—
France	n.a.	+0.46	−0.49	n.a.	—
Poland	+2.96	+1.64	+1.31	—	—
Yugoslavia	+3.90	+3.80	n.a.	—	n.a.
Netherlands	+0.87	−0.21	−1.52	—	—
Hungary	n.a.	+1.66	+1.39	n.a.	—
Belgium[b]	−0.22	−0.83	−1.23	—	—
Bulgaria[c]	n.a.	n.a.	+2.84	n.a.	n.a.
Sweden	+1.92	+1.23	−0.82	—	—
Austria	+0.23	+0.21	+0.13	—	—
Switzerland	+1.92	+1.23	−0.82	—	—
Denmark	+0.04	−0.21	−0.81	—	—

[a] Rome excluded.   [b] Brussels excluded.   [c] 1965–1975.
n.a. = not available.

negative for each period and the decline is accelerating; for the remainder
(France, Netherlands, Sweden, Switzerland, and Denmark) the positive
growth of earlier periods has downturned to become negative, in the course
of the study period.

When the growth rates for the cores of $T_{1-2}-T_{2-3}$ are plotted for
1950–1960 against 1960–1970 ($T_{1-2}-T_{2-3}$) and the rates for 1960–1970
against 1970–1975 ($T_{2-3}-T_{3-4}$) (Fig. 7.1) it is confirmed that all growth rates
are progressively falling (all observations, except Hungary, are above and
to the left of a 45 line) and when the two values are connected for each
country, the negative *direction* of change is clearly shown. What is perhaps
surprising is the *rate* at which the decline occurs.

When the core trends are compared with those of urban rings (Fig. 7.2),
the general contrast is readily apparent. With the exception of Sweden in
the fifties, all countries exhibit a positive growth in rings over the 25 years.
The rates and direction of change do vary considerably, however, particularly from 1950 to 1960. During that period, some six of the eight countries
experienced a rapid rise in ring growth rates. Switzerland, Italy, the
Netherlands, Sweden, and France, for example, had growth rates in excess
of 30 per cent. Denmark and Poland were the only countries to have
declining rates up to 1970 but the growth rates were still in excess of 20 per
cent.

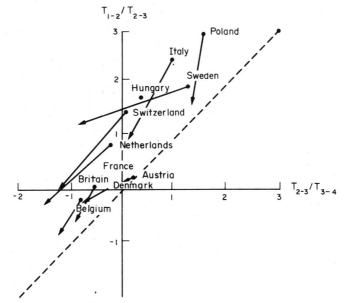

Fig. 7.1. Direction of change in annual growth rates of urban cores, 1950–1975.

After 1970 the trends were more uniform. With the exception of Hungary, all countries had declining growth rates but all remained positive ranging from the Netherlands at 34 per cent (highest) to 5 per cent in Great Britain (lowest).

The ring gains described had the effect of compensating for the core losses in the 1950–1970 period, but after 1970 the relative decline in the rings had the effect of accentuating the core losses, resulting in a general decline in growth rates of FURs in virtually all countries.

A series of tantalizing questions about the implications of such universal trends immediately arises. For example, what interdependent and complementary trends are there within corresponding urban zones (rings), other urban areas, and the rest of the country? What differential effects have changing population growth rates and net migration had on the decline of Europe's central cities? What other economic, social, or policy action has been stimulated or affected by such changes?

For the moment the analysis will be limited to the relation within functional urban regions. From a variety of measures available, just one is chosen at this stage: the share of the core in the total population of the functional urban region. When the ratios are compared through time, a measure of relative centralization (positive shift) or decentralization (negative shift) is derived.

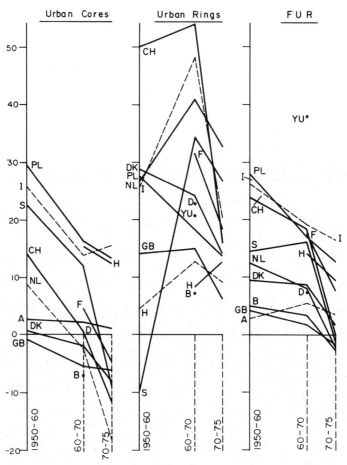

Fig. 7.2. Annual growth rates by urban zone of FURs, 1950–1960, 1960–1970, and 1970–1975.

The share of the core in the total FUR population is given for each country in Table 7.2. The variation in core shares among countries (in 1960 ranging from 38.57 per cent in Belgium to over 80 per cent in Yugoslavia) is partly due to problems related to the delimitation of core–ring boundaries. Given the conclusion to Chapter 6, this was to be expected. However, the variability should not detract from the general conclusion that follows from analysing the *direction of change* in each time period. Once again the tendency is quite unambiguous: in Hungary and Bulgaria the ratios increase over time, which implies strong centralization of the population in the core areas. Although Poland has two positive shifts and one negative, the ratio remains virtually constant throughout the whole period.

TABLE 7.2.
Core share and shift in core share of FUR population by country, 1950–1975

	Dates						
	Core population/Total FUR population (%)				Direction of change		
Country	1950	1960	1970	1975	1950–60	1960–70	1970–75
FRG	n.a.	71.43	69.95	n.a.	n.a.	–	n.a.
Italy	80.64	80.38	75.27	76.10	–	–	+
GB	68.47	64.45	60.71	59.33	–	–	–
France	n.a.	50.96	47.32	43.37	n.a.	–	–
Poland	66.65	67.03	66.64	66.70	+	–	+
Yugoslavia	80.51	80.48	78.27	n.a.	–	–	n.a.
Netherlands	78.70	76.02	68.70	63.05	–	–	–
Hungary	n.a.	74.52	75.93	76.10	n.a.	+	+
Belgium	41.28	38.57	35.04	33.68	–	–	–
Bulgaria	n.a.	n.a.	63.01	69.18	n.a.	n.a.	+
Sweden	77.47	67.87	57.82	54.49	–	–	–
Austria	71.84	71.41	69.33	68.52	–	–	–
Switzerland	73.47	67.87	57.82	54.49	–	–	–
Denmark	65.64	59.81	53.91	51.24	–	–	–

n.a. = not available.

In all other countries the ratios are negative, which implies relative decentralization. In some cases the rate of change is considerable; in Sweden, for example, the share of the cores sank from 77.5 per cent in 1950 to 54.5 per cent in 1975, in Switzerland from 73.5 per cent to 54.5 per cent in the same period.

7.2. Stages of urban development: a classification of FUR

It has therefore proved possible to determine important trends between urban zones and between various groups of countries; it is perhaps more important, however, to determine the precise type of shift which has produced the patterns of centralization and decentralization, particularly on the level of individual functional urban regions. To that end, a classification of all FURs according to the stage of development reached is made below.

Although the classification procedure adopted (see Part I) is based solely upon the criterion of population change between urban zones, it has several advantages.

First, it rests heavily on the assumption that population change is an indicator of the spatial welfare preferences of major decision agents, and thus any changes that can be monitored are a useful surrogate for changes in spatial structure and organization.

Second, it discriminates well between FURs and between countries and is an aid to reducing the diversity of the total sample of FURs to subgroups for further analysis.

Third, the actual procedure has the virtue of simplicity, but not only in operational terms. It is felt that a more complex multivariate classification would make interpretation even more problematic, given the complexity of the processes involved and the heterogeneity of the sample of FURs drawn from so many countries. The strategy is therefore to leave much of the data untransformed and to use a methodology which is essentially descriptive.

The particular measure of centralization–decentralization is based upon a comparison of the differential population change between each urban core and urban ring. This comparison could be based on either absolute or relative population change. However, as urban cores generally have a much larger population than the rings, the use of absolute values might just reflect the imbalance and not the relative importance of change in each urban zone. For this reason, the classification is based upon percentage growth rates.

In practice, the procedure is quite straightforward and involves plotting positive or negative population change of the core against such change in the ring. When considered in the context of total FUR growth or decline, the relative balance of change between the urban zones produces an eight-way classification of development types. These relationships are illustrated graphically in Fig. 7.3.

It could be argued, considering Fig. 7.3, that the countries fall into a continuum as the position of each FUR rotates from absolute centralization to absolute decentralization. Whether or not they do is probably less important than recognizing the apparent "stage" each country has reached and that within this broad categorization there are significant variations, also *between* cities within the same country.

In terms of national stages of urban development, a number of countries are experiencing centralization during the transition stage (Hungary, Bulgaria, and Yugoslavia); other countries are placed in the intermediate position between centralization and decentralization in the transition from Urbanization to Suburbanization (Italy, France, and Denmark), while the remaining countries experience a clear decentralization in the Suburbanization to Desurbanization stage (the Netherlands, Switzerland, Great Britain, and Belgium).

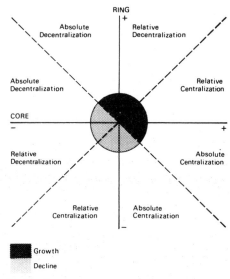

Fig. 7.3. Classification of urban development types.

7.3. Variation in FUR development trends, 1960–1970

The variation by individual FURs within these broad classes reveals some interesting features. All the FURs have been classified and cross-tabulated by urban size (Table 7.3). The results are consistent with the general hypothesis (see Chapter 3) that population centralization–decentralization is related to city size and the level of economic development of

TABLE 7.3.
Percentage population change in FURs by size class and classification type, 1960–1970

Size classes	Classification types					Total	N
	1	2	3	4	5–8		
< ¼ m	24.32	23.24	17.46	7.12	−1.72	15.78	69
¼–½ m	10.59	20.12	13.01	7.85	−1.09	11.77	61
½–1 m		16.08	13.68	7.04	−1.09	11.77	27
1–2 m			18.49	8.87	−2.45	9.97	15
2–5 m			17.30	3.13	−1.25	8.66	7
> 5 m				5.66	−4.28	2.12	3
Total	20.52	19.43	15.56	6.39	−3.08	9.14	182
N	9	28	92	44	12	185	

TABLE 7.4.

FURs classification by stage of development and population size, 1975

Pop. size	Classification types						
	1	2	3	4	5	6	7
1 million	Sofia Warsaw	Marseilles Budapest Turin Katowice		Paris Lyons Birmingham Leeds Milan Stockholm Naples	Vienna Brussels Copenhagen Manchester Glasgow Newcastle Rotterdam Amsterdam	London Liverpool	
½–1 million		Bielsko-Biala Krakow Plovdiv	Poznan Coventry Leicester Palermo Firenze Catania Bari Lodz Gdańsk	Lille Bordeaux Bristol Edinburgh Nottingham Portsmouth Bologna	Antwerp Sheffield Stoke Genoa The Hague Göteborg Zürich		
¼–½ million	Russe St. Etienne Le Havre Debrecen	Varna Miskolc Messina Walbrzych Opole Czestochowa Bydgoszcz	Linz Graz Salzburg Aarhus Toulouse C.-Ferrand Nice Strasbourg Oxford Kielce Luton Slough Plymouth Chatham Verona Brescia Padova Cagliari Taranto Enschede Szczecin Lublin	Nantes Rouen Nancy Teesside Southampton Hull Derby Norwich Motherwell Bolton Venice Utrecht Eindhoven Groningen Geneva Berne Bournemouth Reading	Brighton Trieste Basel Southend	Liège	Sunderland
¼ million	Pleven Stara Zagora Wratza Szeged Györ	Bregenz Burgas Pécs Bialystok Torun Esbjerg	Innsbruck Klagenfurt Odense Aalborg Rennes Montpellier Orleans Dijon Caen Limoges Angers Besançon Cambridge Huddersfield Radom Uppsala Linköping Ipswich Preston	Doncaster Blackpool Wigan Aberdeen Lausanne Lucerne Swansea Västerås	Dundee Winterthur Norrköping	Ghent Charleroi	

the region or country in which the city is located. The following points would seem to substantiate the argument (see Table 7.4):

(i) The earlier stages (types 1 and 2) are dominated by FURs from Eastern European countries.

(ii) The very latest stages of development (types 5–8) are dominated by FURs founded during the Industrial Revolution, e.g. Ghent, Charleroi, Liège, Saarbrücken, Liverpool, Glasgow, Manchester.

(iii) Most capital cities and the larger industrial cities are in a later stage of development than lower-order centres within the same national urban system. For example, Sofia, Budapest, Vienna, Copenhagen, Amsterdam, Zürich, and London all "lead" in their respective nation states.

(iv) The main regional centres in Western Europe are dominantly in types 3 and 4.

7.4. Urban-development stages, 1950–1975

Having identified and confirmed the range of diversity that exists in urban development for the period 1960–1970 and inferred, by a cross-sectional approach, some corroboration for our general theory, we now extend the analysis into a time series (1950–1975) and evaluate in more detail the evolution of the "stages" *within* countries as well as *between* countries.

The method adopted is to classify all FURs within each country by the procedure outlined above and to rank countries according to the dominant stage of urban development. The results for 1950–1960 are given in Table 7.5. It should be noted that only twelve of the possible fourteen countries are included in the classification, owing to data availability, and only Poland is included from Eastern Europe. By summing all FURs in each class, the rows can be expressed in percentages of the total for each country and for the proportions of the whole set of FURs.

The first point of note is the level of growth in the whole sample: some 97 per cent of all cities were growing during the decade. Of these, 47 per cent were in the urbanization stage (types 1 and 2) and 50 per cent were suburbanizing (types 3 and 4). There were marked differences between countries: Sweden, Denmark, Bulgaria, Hungary, and Italy were strongly urbanizing while Switzerland, Great Britain, and Belgium were already suburbanizing. The variability between cities is clearly reflected by some countries having a much wider "spread" of types than others. In Britain, for example, there are FURs in each one of five types, although it is true the distribution is dominated by type 3. In Switzerland, on the other hand, all cities were in type 3. In comparison with the fifties, the classifi-

TABLE 7.5.
Centralization–Decentralization classification of FUR population change by country and dominant stage of urban development, 1950–1960

Dominant stage of urban development	Country	Centralization 1 Abs.	2 Rel.	Decentralization 3 Rel.	4 Abs.	Decentralization 5 Abs.	6 Rel.	Centralization 7 Rel.	8 Abs.	Total %	Total Number of FURs
Urbanization	Sweden	83	17	—	—	—	—	—	—	100	6
	Bulgaria	50	50	—	—	—	—	—	—	100	8
	Denmark	60	20	—	20	—	—	—	—	100	5
	Hungary	17	66	17	—	—	—	—	—	100	6
	Italy	12	70	18	—	—	—	—	—	100	17
Urbanization–Suburbanization	Yugoslavia	—	75	25	—	—	—	—	—	100	8
	Poland	—	53	47	—	—	—	—	—	100	17
	Austria	14	14	71	—	—	—	—	—	100	7
	Netherlands	—	14	86	—	—	—	—	—	100	7
Suburbanization	Switzerland	—	—	100	—	—	—	—	—	100	7
	GB	9	12	53	19	7	—	—	—	100	43
	Belgium	—	—	—	80	20	—	—	—	100	5
Suburbanization–Desurbanization	—	—	—	—	—	—	—	—	—	—	—
Desurbanization	—	—	—	—	—	—	—	—	—	—	—
FURs by type (%)		15	32	40	10	3	0	0	0	100	136

Growth (columns 1–4)   Decline (columns 5–8)

TABLE 7.6.
Centralization–Decentralization classification of FUR population change by country and dominant stage of urban development, 1960–1970

Dominant stage of urban development	Country	Classification types								Total	
		Centralization		Decentralization		Decentralization		Centralization			
		1 Abs.	2 Rel.	3 Rel.	4 Abs.	5 Abs.	6 Rel.	7 Rel.	8 Abs.	%	Number of FURs
Urbanization	Bulgaria	50	50	—	—	—	—	—	—	100	8
	Hungary	66	17	17	—	—	—	—	—	100	6
Urbanization–Suburbanization	Yugoslavia	—	62	38	—	—	—	—	—	100	8
	Sweden	17	50	33	—	—	—	—	—	100	6
	Poland	—	41	59	—	—	—	—	—	100	17
	Italy	—	23	65	12	—	—	—	—	100	17
	Austria	—	14	72	14	—	—	—	—	100	7
	Denmark	—	40	40	20	—	—	—	—	100	5
Suburbanization	France	—	5	68	27	—	—	—	—	100	22
	Switzerland	—	—	57	43	—	—	—	—	100	7
	FRG	—	—	63	33	4	—	—	—	100	27
	Netherlands	—	—	57	29	14	—	—	—	100	7
	GB	—	—	42	44	14	—	—	—	100	43
Suburbanization–Desurbanization	Belgium	—	—	—	40	40	20	—	—	100	5
Desurbanization	—	—	—	—	—	—	—	—	—	—	0
FURs by type (%)		5	15	49	24	6	1	0	0	100	185
		Growth						Decline			

cation for the second time period (1960–1970) is based on a sample of fourteen countries (Table 7.6).

The overall pattern of FUR growth is sustained with 93 per cent of the FURs growing; but the distribution of FURs within the classification shows a greater differentiation. While some 47 per cent of FURs were centralizing in the fifties, the figure had fallen to 20 per cent in the sixties; the corresponding decentralization classes (types 3, 4) had, in contrast, increased from 50 per cent to 73 per cent. The sixties were typically a period of consolidation of the trend towards suburbanization during a period of general FUR growth. Belgium was the only exception, moving strongly from suburbanization to desurbanization.

In the third and final period (1970–1975) the pattern of change had shifted significantly (Table 7.7). By this time, 19 per cent of all FURs were declining and the overall trend was moving inexorably away from centralization. Although type 3 maintained its position as the leading class, as it had throughout the previous two decades, its proportion was now reduced to 34 per cent, while type 4 had risen to 29 per cent. In terms of national changes, the East European countries remained firmly in the urbanization stage, with Poland as the only exception. It maintained a stable position between types 2 and 3 throughout the two and a half decades. Most countries, however, "moved" at least one class. But perhaps the most significant trend to emerge was the *desurbanization* of 15 per cent of all FURs, affecting eight countries. Belgium remained the most desurbanized with all cities in types 5 and 6. The evolution of the European urban system 1960–1970 is represented in Fig. 7.4.

It is now time to draw some interim conclusions from the application of the centralization–decentralization classification.

First, with respect to the general trend for the whole sample of FURs, the shift from centralization towards desurbanization is summarized in Tables 7.8 and 7.9. Between 1950 and 1975 the percentage of FURs in the centralizing classes dropped from 47 per cent to 18 per cent; the suburbanizing classes increased from 50 per cent in the fifties to 73 per cent in the sixties but then declined to 63 per cent in the seventies. Not surprisingly, the desurbanization group (declining cities) reflected these changes by increasing from a meagre 3 per cent in the fifties to 19 per cent in the seventies.

Second, with respect to the national stages of urban development, the classification applied to a time series has revealed important differences between countries (Table 7.10). This summary table classifies each country by stage of development over the three time periods, 1950–1960, 1960–1970, and 1970–1975. Although the number of countries in each time period does vary, the differences are nevertheless indisputable. Of the coun-

TABLE 7.7.

Centralization–Decentralization classification of FUR population change by country and dominant stage of urban development, 1970–1975

Dominant stage of urban development	Country	Centralization		Decentralization		Decentralization		Centralization		Total	
		1 Abs.	2 Rel.	3 Rel.	4 Abs.	5 Abs.	6 Rel.	7 Rel.	8 Abs.	%	Number of FURs
Urbanization	Bulgaria	50	50	—	—	—	—	—	—	100	8
	Hungary	50	33	17	—	—	—	—	—	100	6
Urbanization–Suburbanization	Poland	—	53	41	6	—	—	—	—	100	17
Suburbanization	Austria	9	14	72	—	14	—	—	—	100	7
	France	—	—	59	32	—	—	—	—	100	22
	Italy	—	6	59	23	12	—	—	—	100	17
	Denmark	—	20	60	—	20	—	—	—	100	5
	Sweden	—	—	33	33	33	—	—	—	100	6
Suburbanization–Desurbanization	GB	—	—	21	53	19	5	2	—	100	43
	Netherlands	—	—	14	43	43	—	—	—	100	7
	Switzerland	—	—	—	57	43	—	—	—	100	7
Desurbanization	Belgium	—	—	—	—	40	60	—	—	100	5
FURs by type (%)		6	12	34	29	15	3	1	0	100	150

Growth (columns 1–4) — Decline (columns 5–8)

Classification types

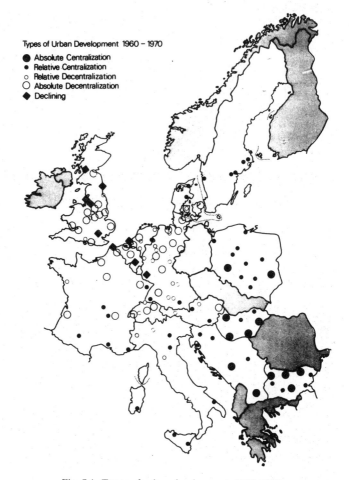

Types of Urban Development 1960 – 1970

● Absolute Centralization
● Relative Centralization
○ Relative Decentralization
○ Absolute Decentralization
◆ Declining

Fig. 7.4. Types of urban development, 1960–1970.

TABLE 7.8.
Proportion of FURs in classification types

	Type								
Date	1	2	3	4	5	6	7	8	Total
1950–1960	15	32	40	10	3	0	0	0	100
1960–1970	5	15	49	24	6	1	0	0	100
1970–1975	6	12	34	29	15	3	1	0	100

TABLE 7.9.

Proportion of FURs in development stages, 1950–1975

	Stage				
Date	Urbanization	Suburbanization	Desurbanization	Reurbanization	Total
1950–1960	47	50	3	0	100
1960–1970	20	73	7	0	100
1970–1975	18	63	18	1	100

tries represented in each time period Bulgaria, Hungary, and Poland are the only ones not to change from one stage of development to another; all other countries moved at least one stage. Sweden, Denmark, Italy, the Netherlands, and Belgium all moved two stages.

The evolutionary nature of the whole European urban system is manifest, but national and individual FUR differences must now be given their just recognition.

TABLE 7.10.

Changes in the classification of countries, by dominant stage of urban development, 1950–1975

Dominant stage	Period		
	1950–1960	1960–1970	1970–1975
Urbanization	Sweden Bulgaria Denmark Hungary Italy	Bulgaria Hungary	Bulgaria Hungary
Urbanization/ Suburbanization	Yugoslavia Poland Austria Netherlands	Yugoslavia Sweden Poland Italy Austria Denmark	Poland
Suburbanization	Switzerland GB Belgium	France Switzerland FRG Netherlands GB	Austria France Italy Denmark Sweden
Suburbanization/ Sesurbanization	—	Belgium	GB Netherlands Switzerland
Desurbanization	—	—	Belgium

7.5. Urban trends in each dominant stage of development

The objective now is to take the three dominant stages of urban development that have been identified and to analyse the group characteristics of the FURs that are in each stage in 1975. The three groups are analysed in terms of the components of population change (natural change and net migration), the growth of employment, and changing employment structure. This temporal analysis by urban zone serves to test some aspects of the general theory and to demonstrate the efficacy of the classification procedure itself.

The outcome of the analysis is presented for each of the three main stages by using a selection of functional urban regions to illustrate the main trends.

Stage I: Urbanization

Urbanization is defined as the stage when either absolute or relative centralization of population is occurring in the core. The theory suggests this to be the outcome of a process of population concentration into the FUR from the rest of the country and even from within the FUR itself, from the incipient hinterland or ring to the core.

These implied population movements can be shown by analysing the components of population change over the periods 1960–1970 and 1970–1975 and by assessing their relative importance (Table 7.11). The growth rates reveal several clear trends:

(i) natural change is positive in virtually all cores and rings for both time periods, and frequently higher in the cores than the rings, particularly after 1970;

(ii) core natural-change rates are consistently lower than core net-migration rates;

(iii) net migration is positive in the cores for both periods and is significantly more important than natural change in accounting for population change;

(iv) net migration is generally negative in the rings. For type 1 FURs, all population losses are due to negative net migration that is greater than natural-change increases. It is this phenomenon that accounts for absolute centralization. For type 2 FURs, the trends are similar but the net migration is lower than natural change and therefore relative centralization occurs instead. The question arises what economic and social forces are generating such trends. It was argued earlier that a link exists between the "stages" and the level of development; if that is the case, it should be possible to identify a

TABLE 7.11.
Components of population change, 1960–1970–1975, for selected FURs in classification types 1 and 2

Classification types	FUR and country		Components of population change, 1960-1970					Components of population change, 1970-1975				
			Total of change FUR	Natural change		Net migration		Total of change FUR	Natural change		Net migration	
				Core	Ring	Core	Ring		Core	Ring	Core	Ring
Type 1 Absolute centralization	Vratza	BG	10.56	3.54	4.27	11.63	-8.88	6.58	3.01	-0.87	7.17	-0.73
	Russe	BG	18.72	4.24	3.73	16.36	-4.61	4.88	3.21	0.17	3.15	-1.66
	Debrecen	H	8.75	2.57	4.11	9.52	-7.45	8.82	3.33	2.15	7.59	-4.06
	Szeged	H	14.49	0.26	1.24	28.57	-15.58	9.01	2.37	0.24	7.51	-1.11
	Serajevo	YU	38.89	10.92	9.58	37.90	-19.53	n.a.	n.a.	n.a.	n.a.	n.a.
Type 2 Relative centralization	Sofia	BG	20.22	4.75	1.64	13.96	-0.13	7.39	3.93	0.22	3.38	-0.14
	Varna	BG	33.43	4.85	2.71	26.72	-0.35	13.30	5.03	1.22	7.19	-0.14
	Miskolc	H	12.15	3.36	4.93	9.89	-6.04	6.97	2.67	2.34	4.11	-2.15
	Zagreb	YU	30.66	7.16	0.42	22.40	0.57	n.a.	n.a.	n.a.	n.a.	n.a.
	Ljubljana	YU	29.02	8.93	1.79	15.68	2.60	n.a.	n.a.	n.a.	n.a.	n.a.

n.a. = not available.

TABLE 7.12.
Total employment change by sector, 1960–1970, for selected FURs in classification types 1 and 2

Classification types	FUR and country		Core				Ring				Total			
			Industry	Services	Other sectors	Total	Industry	Services	Other sectors	Total	Industry	Services	Other sectors	Total
Type 1 Absolute centralization	Vratza	BG	10.20	10.40	6.52	27.12	0.27	0.15	−14.33	−13.91	10.47	10.55	−7.81	13.21
	Russe	BG	9.60	11.76	−4.59	16.77	0.11	0.55	−10.79	−10.13	9.71	12.31	−15.38	6.64
	Debrecen	H	10.64	5.45	0.29	16.38	3.13	1.00	−11.35	−7.22	13.77	6.45	−11.06	9.16
	Szeged	H	6.68	2.74	2.13	11.55	6.19	1.75	−10.23	−2.29	12.88	4.49	−8.11	9.26
	Serajevo	YU				48.13				−11.77				36.37
Type 2 Relative centralization	Sofia	BG	−0.20	18.77	4.28	22.85	1.36	3.07	−4.00	0.43	1.16	22.84	0.28	24.28
	Varna	BG	13.81	17.72	7.69	39.22	1.16	1.51	−0.54	2.13	14.98	19.23	7.14	41.35
	Miskolc	H	7.13	6.09	1.72	14.94	5.63	1.15	−9.53	−2.75	12.77	7.24	−7.82	12.19
	Zagreb	YU				29.32				10.45				39.78
	Ljubljana	YU				63.22				5.62				68.84

(Editorial note: data for three Yugoslavian FURs being re-analysed).

TABLE 7.13.

Components of population change, 1960–1970–1975, for selected FURs in classification types 3 and 4

Classification types	FUR and country		Components of population change, 1960–1970					Components of population change, 1970–1975				
			Total change FUR	Natural change		Net migration		Total change FUR	Natural change		Net migration	
				Core	Ring	Core	Ring		Core	Ring	Core	Ring
Type 3 Relative decentralization	Budapest	H	14.60	−0.87	0.74	11.53	3.19	6.12	0.20	0.95	3.15	1.73
	Turin	I	28.80	5.56	3.16	5.59	14.48	3.54	1.77	1.45	−0.94	1.27
	Cagliari	I	23.42	14.39	5.70	1.93	1.40	11.56	5.09	2.60	1.06	2.81
	Toulouse	F	20.32	4.63	0.68	8.25	6.76	12.61	4.15	1.79	−3.49	10.17
	Dijon	F	17.79	5.65	1.50	0.53	10.10	10.41	6.00	2.64	−2.60	4.37
	Salzburg	A	18.28	2.46	6.40	7.20	2.22	8.35	0.32	1.79	3.68	2.56
	Innsbruck	A	18.65	2.51	7.21	5.25	3.69	7.07	0.30	2.32	2.03	2.42
	Odense	DK	20.76	6.69	2.75	2.14	9.19	4.07	2.45	0.95	−0.80	1.48
	Belgrade	YU	34.83	9.31	0.57	17.56	7.59	n.a.	n.a.	n.a.	n.a.	n.a.
	Luton	GB	21.50	2.15	6.21	8.78	4.37	4.18	n.a.	n.a.	n.a.	n.a.
Type 4 Absolute decentralization	Milan	I	24.57	3.96	4.88	3.19	12.54	2.82	0.71	1.95	−1.70	1.85
	Naples	I	12.54	10.65	6.77	−8.11	3.23	5.18	3.47	3.49	−3.68	1.90
	Paris	F	8.09	0.99	3.76	−3.63	6.96	2.77	0.82	4.70	−4.37	1.63
	Bordeaux	F	11.38	1.34	2.13	−3.70	11.61	6.54	1.19	3.34	−9.03	11.03
	Birmingham	GB	4.56	5.28	3.13	−8.57	4.72	0.13	n.a.	n.a.	n.a.	n.a.
	Leeds	GB	3.70	3.78	1.57	−5.30	3.65	0.21	n.a.	n.a.	n.a.	n.a.
	Bristol	GB	8.86	3.41	2.92	−4.31	6.84	0.92	n.a.	n.a.	n.a.	n.a.
	Eindhoven	NL	26.35	7.38	12.52	−0.60	7.05	7.72	1.62	4.01	−2.45	4.54
	Utrecht	NL	17.73	7.91	5.40	−1.28	5.70	1.36	2.18	5.24	−3.82	1.72
	Berne	CH	14.90	2.04	5.79	−2.35	9.42	0.37	−0.20	2.16	−3.57	1.80
	Lausanne	CH	24.91	2.41	4.38	3.66	14.46	1.20	0.38	2.06	−1.30	0.05

n.a. = not available.

Total employment change by sector, 1960–1970,

Classification types	FUR and country		Core			
			Industry	Services	Other sectors	Total
Type 3 Relative decentralization	Budapest	H	2.23	3.66	2.14	8.03
	Turin	I	−4.11	3.25	−0.81	−1.67
	Cagliari	I	3.68	13.05	7.54	24.27
	Salzburg	A	1.32	9.78	−0.36	10.74
	Innsbruck	A	0.28	7.13	−0.32	7.09
	Odense	DK	4.55	23.99	−17.89	10.65
	Belgrade	YU				24.05
	Luton	GB				
Type 4 Absolute decentralization	Milan	I	−7.99	6.30	2.15	0.46
	Naples	I	−1.87	−0.82	−0.27	−2.96
	Birmingham	GB				−4.93
	Leeds	GB				−6.50
	Bristol	GB				2.31
	Eindhoven	NL	5.90	9.03	0.88	15.81
	Utrecht	NL	−4.93	25.59	0.02	20.68
	Berne	CH	1.85	13.55	−0.17	15.23
	Lausanne	CH	0.54	15.47	−0.19	15.82

(Editorial note: data for one Yugoslavian and four British FURs being re-analysed.)

relationship between the changes of population and those of employment.

In both types 1 and 2, employment growth occurred between 1960 and 1970 in all FURs (Table 7.12) but there were differences in employment-growth rates between the cores and the rings, suggesting a high correlation between population and employment change, even on the level of the urban zone.

In type 1, the growth of jobs in the core was between 11 and 48 per cent, while all the rings declined absolutely in terms of employment. The same pattern of core job growth is also apparent in type 2 FURs, but these cities were in a stage of relative centralization and that is reflected by ring employment growth, albeit mostly at a lower rate of increase than in the cores. The close relationship between population and employment growth rates implied above is actually borne out when the two variables are correlated for each urban zone.

Correlation of population change with employment change, 1960–1970

	Core	Ring	FUR
$r =$	0.82	0.96	0.99

7.14.
for selected FURs in classification types 3 and 4

Ring				Total			
Industry	Services	Other sectors	Total	Industry	Services	Other sectors	Total
0.94	1.00	2.35	4.29	3.17	4.67	4.52	12.32
9.23	2.25	0.06	11.54	5.13	5.50	−0.75	9.87
0.28	2.32	0.0	2.60	3.96	15.37	7.54	26.87
3.60	2.69	−4.15	2.14	4.93	12.47	−4.51	12.88
1.10	3.25	−4.01	0.34	1.39	10.38	−4.33	7.42
19.29	15.64	−21.15	13.78	23.84	39.63	−39.04	24.43
			3.16				27.21
4.77	2.97	0.23	7.97	−3.22	9.27	2.40	8.44
5.29	2.67	−0.36	7.60	3.41	1.85	−0.63	4.64
			5.07				0.14
			2.40				−4.18
			6.38				8.49
1.43	6.12	1.67	9.22	7.33	15.16	2.55	25.03
1.86	6.46	1.38	9.70	−3.07	32.05	1.40	30.38
3.55	4.43	−0.24	7.74	5.40	17.98	−0.41	22.98
10.57	5.76	1.30	17.63	11.11	21.23	1.11	33.45

In terms of changing employment structure, there is a strong commitment in all FURs (with the exception of Sofia) to industrial growth (from 6 per cent to 13 per cent) but it is interesting to note that this occurs simultaneously with comparable increases in service-sector jobs. It is worth reflecting on this trend, as all the FURs in this stage are located in Eastern Europe. While the urbanization of Western Europe was characterized by industrial growth preceding the growth of tertiary employment, it would appear that urbanization in Eastern Europe is occurring not only within a different social milieu but also in a quite different historical context. The level of technological diffusion, population mobility, and economic interdependencies are markedly different from those pertaining during the industrial revolution of Western countries.

Stage 2: Suburbanization

Suburbanization is defined as the stage when either relative or absolute decentralization of population is taking place in the core. Within that general framework, the sample of FURs in types 3 and 4 vary considerably in their size and function, and come from eight countries.

The relative importance of the two components of population change are examined first. As with the Urbanization stage, natural change remains positive in both urban zones. But in the Suburbanization stage the rates are consistently higher in the rings and undoubtedly contribute strongly to the growth performance in these zones. That is considerably reinforced by net migration in the rings (Table 7.13).

Suburbanization implies overall growth with an outward dispersal of population over time, which leads to weaker growth performance and eventual decline of core areas. That notion is borne out in type 3, where corresponding low growth rates are to be found in the cores with a trend towards negative rates. The same is achieved in type 4 where the many negative rates in the 1960s are followed by all cores suffering negative net migration in the 1970–1975 period.

Net-migration gains and losses in cores and rings, respectively, are the main determinants of the Suburbanization stage. The trend is universal, despite the wide variety of city sizes, locations, functions, and nation states.

During the Suburbanization stage, employment growth is generally strong in all urban zones. It is true that some large city cores (Turin, Naples, Birmingham, and Leeds) show small declines, but for the others, the rates of increase vary between 1 and 25 per cent in both types 3 and 4. This is in marked contrast to the core changes in population, where the demographic losses were not matched by a commensurate loss in employment. The lagged response has many policy implications, none more so than the likely increase in demand for interzonal commuting as the labour market will achieve its own equilibrium through longer work journeys.

Such problems are compounded when the effect of changing employment structure is considered. The trends are clear enough (Table 7.14). For FURs in type 3, service-employment growth is consistently higher than industrial growth, particularly in core areas. Industrial-employment growth is positive in the rings together with tertiary employment, the latter often tied to the needs of the local population.

For those FURs in type 4, the decline in industrial employment in the core is much more apparent and is actually negative in many cases. In contrast, the growth of service employment remains strongly rooted in the core and to a lesser extent in the rings. If the decline in population is matched by decline in industrial employment in these type 4 FURs, it is occurring at a time when service jobs are strongly centralizing.

Stage 3: Desurbanization

Desurbanization is defined as the stage when the whole FUR is declining in total population, with the rings still gaining (type 5), and then all zones declining (type 6). The examples selected here are taken from six countries and it can be seen that, with few exceptions, the sample of FURs is a very

TABLE 7.15.
Components of population change, 1960–1970–1975, for selected FURs in classification types 5–7

Classification types	FUR and country		Components of population change, 1960–1970					Components of population change, 1970–1975				
			Total change FUR	Natural change Core	Ring	Net migration Core	Ring	Total change FUR	Natural change Core	Ring	Net migration Core	Ring
Type 5 Absolute decentralization during decline	Vienna	A	0.63	-3.72	0.20	3.10	1.05	-0.32	-2.98	-0.37	2.43	0.60
	Copenhagen	DK	4.61	-0.17	4.95	-6.87	6.71	-0.70	-0.70	2.14	-3.42	1.28
	Rotterdam	NL	8.94	7.56	4.21	-10.90	8.07	-2.31	0.40	2.10	-7.98	3.16
	Amsterdam	NL	3.31	5.51	3.41	-10.18	4.58	-4.17	-0.16	1.20	-7.03	1.82
	The Hague	NL	-1.77	4.53	3.15	-13.23	3.77	-4.29	-0.77	1.29	-7.95	3.14
	Zürich	CH	14.18	1.67	6.14	-4.45	10.82	-0.68	-0.60	1.50	-3.13	1.55
	Basel	CH	17.23	2.21	5.57	-0.33	9.78	-1.64	-0.35	1.33	-4.18	1.55
	Glasgow	GB	-2.33	5.61	2.60	-14.96	4.43	-3.30	n.a.	n.a.	n.a.	n.a.
	Manchester	GB	-1.25	3.22	2.09	-11.03	4.47	-1.35	n.a.	n.a.	n.a.	n.a.
	Newcastle	GB	-1.30	2.58	2.03	-9.31	3.40	-0.99	n.a.	n.a.	n.a.	n.a.
	Sheffield	GB	1.02	3.32	2.37	-5.26	0.59	-0.23	n.a.	n.a.	n.a.	n.a.
	Brussels	B	5.64	n.a.	n.a.	n.a.	n.a.	-1.91	n.a.	n.a.	n.a.	n.a.
	Antwerp	B	4.15	-0.34	4.76	-4.31	4.54	-1.60	-0.63	0.30	-1.95	0.68
Types 6 & 7 Relative decentralization during decline	London	GB	-4.29	3.60	2.07	-9.60	-0.36	-3.16	n.a.	n.a.	n.a.	n.a.
	Liverpool	GB	-3.37	4.92	2.27	-14.05	3.49	-4.04	n.a.	n.a.	n.a.	n.a.
	Sunderland	GB	-0.81	1.23	3.00	-1.80	-3.24	-1.95	n.a.	n.a.	n.a.	n.a.
	Liège	B	-1.24	-0.71	-0.54	-1.01	1.03	-2.51	-0.51	-0.40	-1.28	-0.31
	Charleroi	B	-1.72	-0.06	-0.05	-0.92	-0.70	-3.49	-0.07	-0.16	-0.68	-2.58

n.a. = not available.

TABLE
Total employment change by sector, 1960–1970,

Classification types	FUR and country		Core			
			Industry	Services	Other sectors	Total
Type 5	Vienna	A	−10.07	2.53	−0.19	−7.73
Absolute	Copenhagen	DK				−8.67
decentralization	Rotterdam	NL	−4.56	9.04	−1.43	3.05
during decline	Amsterdam	NL	−9.18	11.38	−1.37	0.83
	The Hague	NL	−4.63	−0.20	−2.44	−7.27
	Zürich	CH	−1.73	11.26	−0.12	9.41
	Basel	CH	3.40	8.40	−0.05	11.75
	Glasgow	GB				−12.74
	Manchester	GB				−10.43
	Newcastle	GB				−5.90
	Sheffield	GB				−1.93
	Brussels	B	n.a.	n.a.	n.a.	n.a.
	Antwerp	B	1.20	−0.82	0.38	0.76
Types 6 & 7	London	GB				
Relative	Liverpool	GB				
decentralization	Sunderland	GB				
during decline	Liège	B	−4.83	3.49	−0.17	−1.51
	Charleroi	B	0.36	1.90	−0.60	1.66

(Editorial note: data for seven British FURs being re-analysed.)
n.a. = not available.

distinctive one. It includes many of Europe's leading cities, capitals, ports, and old industrial centres.

The total-population decline of these cities is largely attributable to the extensive losses of population in the core areas. Between 1960 and 1970 it was largely due to net-migration losses, but by 1970–1975 there were additional losses due to negative natural-change rates. Population growth in the rings by natural change and net migration was sufficient to offset many of these core losses in the sixties, but by 1975 decreases in the rates of growth of both components in the rings resulted in overall FUR decline. In type 6 the data after 1970 are incomplete, but those available for Belgian cities suggest a total decline in both components for *all* urban zones.

With employment data only available for the 1960–1970 period, the full impact of these dramatic population losses are difficult to assess. It does appear, however, that some important differences in employment change have occurred between countries. For the industrial centres in Britain, Vienna, Copenhagen, and The Hague the trends are similar (see Tables 7.15 and 7.16): heavy losses of jobs in the core, growth in the ring, and some losses in the FUR overall. But in the cores of some Dutch and Swiss cities job losses show a time lag, compared with population losses. In fact,

7.16.
for selected FURs in classification groups 5–7

Ring				Total			
Industry	Services	Other sectors	Total	Industry	Services	Other sectors	Total
0.18	1.04	−1.49	−0.27	−9.89	3.57	−1.68	−8.00
			15.85				7.18
1.12	3.72	1.26	6.10	−3.44	12.76	−0.17	9.15
1.35	6.82	0.80	8.97	−7.83	18.20	−0.57	9.80
−0.16	6.10	1.44	7.38	−4.79	5.90	−1.00	0.11
5.15	6.92	−0.38	11.69	3.42	18.18	−0.50	21.11
4.34	3.63	0.33	8.30	7.74	12.02	0.27	20.04
			4.91				−7.82
			2.46				−7.97
			5.39				−0.50
			−1.59				−3.52
n.a.	n.a.	n.a.	n.a.	−7.49	7.67	3.92	4.10
−0.81	3.60	1.35	4.14	0.39	2.78	1.73	4.90
−8.07	1.14	−0.56	−7.49	−12.90	4.63	−0.73	−9.0
−11.12	2.59	0.83	−7.70	−10.77	4.50	0.23	−6.04

Rotterdam, Amsterdam, Zürich, and Basel all experienced a core increase in employment, with the two Swiss cities growing 10 and 12 per cent respectively. Ring growth was also strong. The Belgian cities vary considerably; Brussels and Antwerp experience the lagged-growth effect, but the FURs in the Belgian coalfield are declining overall although Charleroi has employment growth in the core.

For those FURs where employment-structure data are available, there is a greater consistency. The general core decline in industrial employment and service growth is to be found in most FURs. Growth of both industry and services occurs strongly in the rings.

7.6. Summary

The foregoing considerations lead to the conclusion that the theory of urban development presented in Part I of this volume seems an efficient tool for analysing actual urban developments. The available data seem to confirm the main hypothesis. The three stages: urbanization, suburbanisation, and desurbanization, could be clearly identified.

Uncertainty remains concerning the reurbanization stage. Is reurbanization only possible through intensive action on the part of the local or regional authorities, or is it a stage "naturally" following that of desurbanization?

Further information, for which, unfortunately, we shall have to wait patiently, will give us more insight into this problem. In Chapter 3 it has already been indicated that cities in earlier stages would do well to concentrate on measures that could prevent their entering into the stage of desurbanization, as in this stage the very existence of their urban area is in jeopardy.

PART III

Elements of a Theory on Urban
Policy and an Evaluation of
National Urban Policies in Europe

8

Introduction

In Chapter 7 we have seen that urban systems evolve according to a general pattern. Urban growth is followed by urban sprawl and ends in urban decline. In Part I the government has been considered as one of the agents whose actions can influence the urban development pattern.

The government was presented there as serving the general interest, its task being to govern the locational behaviour of individual households and industries by dint of regulation and stimulation in such a way that everybody achieves optimum well-being, given, of course, certain objective constraints and historical inflexibilities. So, the fundamental question of policy to be answered is: should the government accept the urban spatial developments described before as exogenously given and, as a consequence, take only measures that follow the process and solve problems "at the margin", or should it try to influence the locational behaviour of the three groups concerned (households, companies, and government authorities) in such a way that urban development from a welfare point of view will be optimum in the long run?

In our view, we must opt for the latter alternative. From the discussion of traffic problems in various stages of urban development it has already become apparent that government action can greatly influence the further evolution of the spatial pattern of towns, and also that this influence can be detrimental if government measures take insufficient account of external effects.

The purpose of Part III is to gain some insight into the way governments may have determined the national urban development patterns that have been described in Part II.

Before evaluating national urban policies, however, we shall present a theory of urban policy. In Part I we have already given a general exposé of the role the government plays in the urbanization process. In Chapter 9 we shall deal more explicitly with the position and function of urban policy in order to establish a structured framework within which to place and evaluate the national urban policies of the various countries in Chapters 11 and 12.

9

A Theory of Urban Policy

9.1. What is urban policy?

The term "urban policy" simply means "town-oriented policy" as distinguished from non-urban or rural, regional, and national policy. All these terms merely indicate the geographical range of the policy; they do not say anything about its content (economic, housing, or traffic policy, for instance), nor do they indicate the authority which is responsible for it (national, regional, or local government). In practice, however, "urban policy" is generally understood to involve the whole body of government measures at different administrative levels which aim to influence and regulate urbanization in such a way that its outcome is in agreement with the government's objectives.

The dimensions of "process—objectives—measures" are typical of all forms of governmental policy. Applied to urban policy its logical build up may be represented schematically as shown in Fig. 9.1.

Figure 9.1 shows that the urban system is subject to changes as a consequence of discrepancies which can occur in one or more fields which the system cannot solve of its own accord. The government is then supposed to intervene to steer the process along the right track.

In fact, it is in the confrontation between the actual state of the urban system as the government perceives it and the state the government desires for it in view of its own values and preferences that problems are revealed and can be identified.

The formulation of objectives follows the identification of problems. The term "objectives" is used here in the narrow sense of "targets", i.e. formulation of the more general goals or aims that represent the elements of a desired state, and that are often also called "objectives". An example may clarify the difference. If the government wishes that everybody can afford a good house, while an evaluation of the real situation reveals a housing shortage, the government's specific objective (target) will be the construction of houses of a certain quality and price.

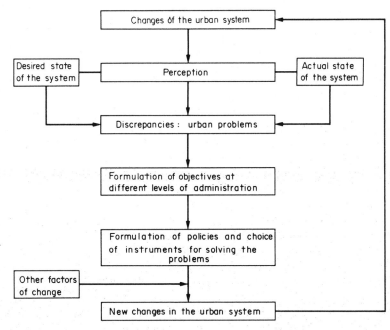

Fig. 9.1. The process of urban planning.

The last step in the government's action is the preparation and implementation of measures to realize objectives and so to solve problems. These policy measures together with other factors will cause new changes in the urban system, so that the process starts again from the beginning; it is clearly a cyclical process.

Figure 9.1 does not include the content of different measures of urban policy, nor the way in which nor the relationships through which the policies are supposed to influence the urban system. This system is an extremely complicated one, but, it may be useful to study at any rate the more important relationships by means of an, admittedly simplified, scheme. An example of this is Fig. 9.2. It should be read as follows:

The cells in the second row together with the middle cell in the fourth row represent the elements that are essential for the well-being of the individual household. They are:

System I

   A. 1. Number, quality, and location of jobs.
      2. Size, quality, and location of recreation areas.

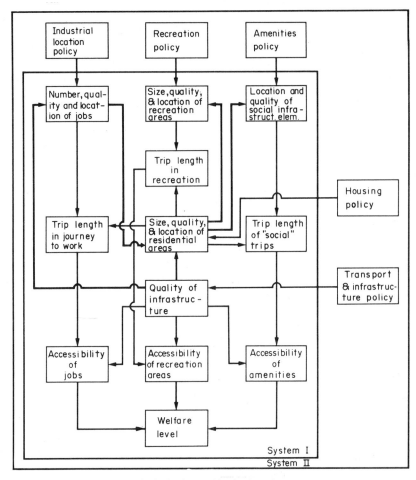

Fig. 9.2. Principal relationships in the urban system.

3. Location and quality of social infrastructure elements.
4. Size, quality, and location of residential areas.

These four cells represent the elements that are decisive for the quality of life of an individual. The location of the first three in relation to the fourth determines the average trip length that a member of a household has to travel to consume the services produced or to reach a certain work place.

B. The trip lengths (three in number) are represented by the cell in the third row and the left-hand and right-hand cells in the fourth row (System I).

Together with the location structure, trip lengths determine, in combination with the quality of the infrastructure, for each household the accessibility of each welfare element. Obviously, although only one system is represented, there are, in fact, more systems, inasmuch as different social and income groups of the population behave in different ways. For some groups some elements might be considerably more important than for others. For old-age pensioners the labour market is of no interest, while households with children take a particular interest in the location and quality of schools, etc.

C. The accessibility of jobs, recreation areas, and amenities, measured from the residential location, together determine the welfare level of the population.

D. Within the system important interrelationships should be considered.

One of them is the influence that the quality of the infrastructure has on the location of the residential areas. The better the infrastructure for private and public transport in the city, the freer the population is to live elsewhere. A very good public transport system allows for a dispersed city with residential areas even in neighbouring municipalities.

A second important relationship is that between the quality of the infrastructure and the location of industrial and service activities. Because for these activities the transportation of goods and raw materials as well as of workers is important, a good transport system allows for greater freedom in the location of firms than a deficient one.

A third interrelationship is that between the locations of jobs and of residential areas. The journey to work is an important consideration for the individual worker, so location of the job is an important factor in determining the location of a household.

Two further relationships represent the fact that, because demands for recreation and for elements of social infrastructure manifest themselves primarily in the neighbourhood of residential areas, it may be assumed that the location of these elements is influenced by the location of residential areas.

System II

Urban policy in the widest sense of the word must be directly or indirectly concerned with all the interdependent elements mentioned in System I. This means that urban policy is composed of a large number of sub-policies associated with the different elements of the urban system. The most important ones are included in System II of the scheme. Listed horizontally are industrial location policy, recreation policy, and amenities policy; listed vertically are housing policy and transportation and infra-structure policy. All these policies influence the elements in System I in one way or another.

A clarification is necessary of certain distinctions made in urban policy between different policy sectors, such as housing, working, recreation, transport. As society becomes more and more complex, government administration has become increasingly specialized with large numbers of departments and agencies each taking responsibility for a separate sector of government administration. This fragmentation is understandable in view of the complexity of the problems to be solved, but it does carry the risk that the essential interdependency of all sub-sectors will be overlooked and that instead of an *integrated urban policy* only *partial* policies will be pursued by independent departments, which each look at and take measures to deal with their own sectors alone, without taking into account the (often negative) effect they might have on other policy sectors. A good example of the strong interaction between the elements of the urban system is presented by Mesarovic and Reisman,[1] who express the opinion that the solution to many critical urban problems depends precisely upon our ability to recognize the complexity of the urban system in an explicit way so that solutions are sought with reference to all relevant influences. They say:

> In order to solve the traffic-congestion problem, the City of London, England, has introduced a new traffic pattern considerably increasing the number of one-way streets and creating many new dead-end streets. In response to requests from residents it also restricted street parking to residents only. The response to the change was very fast and not quite as expected. A working class neighbourhood near the West End was transformed from a noisy, congested area with declining Victorian housing into a quiet urban retreat minutes away from the city-centre. First shop-keepers complained about the increased difficulty in making deliveries. Later, the residents showed concern because of delays in ambulance, policy and other services. But the greatest impact came from the action of developers and speculators. Rents rocketed, the upper middle class began to move in while working class residents were forced to move further away thus further affecting trade and subsequently the entire living pattern. The protests and complaints were quite loud and the City is considering what action to take. At any rate a simple action requiring minimal investment has greatly affected the social structure of the area.

So, the action designed to help local residents was counter-productive or, in our terms, no part of an integrated policy; it forced them away.

A distinction related to that between integrated and partial policy exists also between *explicit* urban policy and *implicit* urban policy. We speak of explicit urban policy when for each relevant policy measure all direct and indirect effects on the various elements of the urban system are weighted. Such an explicit policy is possible only when the objectives at which the measures are directed are formulated consistently and in accordance with

---

[1] Mesarovic and Reisman (1972), *Systems Approval and the City*.

one another. An implicit urban policy, on the contrary, has no such consistency. The word "implicit" means that the (partial) policy is only directed to a sub-sector and is intended to realize only a restricted objective, which is not seen in relation to all other interdependent elements of the urban system. We could take as an example a housing policy that does not consider the location of places of work nor the effect on traffic and road capacity of commuter travel. And yet, because of these interrelationships, these effects materialize. An implicit urban policy rarely furthers the general welfare of a city.

Sub-policies are not only pursued by different departments of the relevant government, they are also realized at different administrative *levels of government*. For instance, amenities policy and infrastructure policy might be carried out, partly at any rate, at a provincial- or central-government level (the educational system, subsidies to public transport, national and provincial road networks, etc.) and partly at a local level.

It seems to be a political matter whether urban policy at a certain level should be controlled and implemented by a government authority at the same level. In some countries, policy-making as well as policy implementation are largely in the hands of the central government; in others, where government is more decentralized, regional and local authorities are in control of most issues. Ideally, it seems to us that the lower level government bodies should have responsibility for the areas concerned with specific problems. Issues of mainly local interest can best be solved at a local level, where the local situation, local preference, and desires are well known and where opportunities for participation by the local population are greater. An essential pre-condition for delegation seems to be an understanding of the relationship between local problems and issues on a higher level, so that the higher authority can determine the limits within which the lower authority has freedom of action, as well as of general policy aims which determine all governmental policies and to which the lower levels of government are party.

As a preliminary conclusion, it should be stressed that for a properly integrated urban policy, aiming at optimizing the welfare level in cities, *coordination* in the horizontal as well as in the vertical direction, i.e. between policy sectors and between policy levels, is essential. Lack of such coordination too often results in contradictory policies within cities. To give an example, an infrastructure policy that aims at improving the transport system of a city will stimulate the growth of the city in the suburbs and in neighbouring municipalities, although the improved system may originally have been intended to facilitate travel from the existing residential areas to the city centre as the centre of employment. If simultaneously a housing policy is pursued that tries to strengthen the residential function of the city centre, these two policies are contradictory and inconsistent. It seems that such a contradiction has become one of the essential features of urban policy in European countries.

9.2. Components of urban policy

Having stressed on the one hand the multiple nature of urban policy, and the need for coordination between the various components of urban policy on the other, we must now examine some of the measures and instruments available. As has been said before the most important activities involved in urbanization are, presumably, living and working. The development of an urban policy can be traced back to the problems arising when the two activities evolve unharmoniously. In practice, urban policy will in most cases be primarily concerned with the spatial organization of living, i.e. with the actual residential pattern of the population; policy-makers will try to find out how all the other components can help to realize a certain desired location pattern on a national, regional, and local scale, and relationships will be between the housing policy on the one hand and the policies of employment location, infrastructure, traffic and transport, environment, recreation, and welfare amenities on the other.

In an urban policy, all those separate policies and their related measures can be seen as the *instruments* for obtaining the desired settlement pattern, instruments derived from each of the policy sectors distinguished. In other words, urban policy has to be put into effect by the simultaneous and coordinated application of measures concerned with house building, amenities, employment, traffic environment, recreation, etc. These instruments can be classified as legal, administrative, or financial. They may either apply to all towns in general or focus on a certain category of towns; examples of the former are measures of administrative reform; of the latter, measures to implement a new-town policy.

In line with our argument that policy measures are the government's answer to certain problems arising from spatial changes, a connection will now be assumed between the nature of urban-policy measures and the successive stages of urban development as distinguished earlier, viz. urbanization, suburbanization, and desurbanization. It may be expected that each stage is attended by a number of clearly distinguishable urban problems, for which the policy-maker has to find a solution. According to Fig. 9.1, the gravity of the problems and the direction in which solutions are sought are determined by the *objectives* of the government, which in turn are derived from the values, preferences, and wishes held by society concerning the most desirable way of urban life. Therefore, it does not follow that each country should take the same sort of measures for the same sort of problem. An evaluation of urban policies in different countries will give us some insight into the differences.

Nevertheless, for the sake of the argument, a connection is supposed between the development stages reached and the policy measures taken. It is to be supposed also that a country passing from one stage to another switches to the new policies belonging to the new stage. The results have been brought together in Table 9.4, "Urban policy instruments for stages of urbanization". This scheme is preceded by three others, viz. Table 9.1, "Spatial developments in stages of urban development", Table 9.2, "Problems connected with spatial developments in stages of urbanization", and Table 9.3, "Objectives of urban policy for stages of urbanization". These schemes summarize the issues dealt with in Part I. The logic behind them is that, according to the argument in Fig. 9.1, problems in one stage are supposed to call forth policy measures that contribute to spatial developments in the next stage, where again problems will arise involving their own policies. The choice of policy measures is determined by the objectives pursued by the government, which express the discrepancies between the actual and the desired state of the urban system. It is the cyclical process pointed out in the previous paragraph that is illustrated here.

From Fig. 9.1 it is apparent that urban policy is conceived as a function of the discrepancies between the desired level of well-being--the objectives—and the actual state of affairs. The aim is, of course, to minimize the weighted sum of discrepancies with the help of a suitable set of instruments. The weights to be given depend on the preferences ascribed to the relevant policy areas.

Now if such discrepancies do indeed largely determine urban policy, the logical question is how to acquire an understanding of their size.

First of all a policy-maker can try and assess the differences between the desired and the actual level of policy-relevant components of the urban system. An urban policy based on that difference will always be an *ad-hoc* policy; the situation is illustrated by Tables 9.1 to 9.4. To give an example: a policy-maker charged with adjusting the development of a functional urban area in the suburbanization phase will act as follows:

(a) He will analyse the objective, as indicated in column 2 of Table 9.3.
(b) He will analyse developments, as indicated in column 2 of Table 9.1.
(c) From a confrontation of (a) and (b) he will derive discrepancies such as reproduced in column 2 of Table 9.2.

In line with his attitude towards policy, our policy-maker will decide to use the tools mentioned in column 2 of Table 9.4. Needless to say such a policy tends to cure rather than prevent urban problems.

TABLE 9.1.

Spatial developments in stages of urban development

Developments in the sphere of	Urban development stages		
	Urbanization	Suburbanization	Desurbanization and inter-urban decentralization
Working	Construction of industrial productive capacity in the cores Forming of industrial complexes Attraction of labour from the country to the city core Lagging behind of rural areas Functional specialization of cores or parts of cores: manufacturing, commerce, administration, etc. Stagnation of intermediate towns	Further expansion and modernization of industry, together with relocation of factories out of city centres Stronger relations between rural and urban economic systems New industrial technologies promote further concentration of industries Nation-wide electrification Rise of central business district with large offices and shopping centres Decline of urban-rural distinction Further mechanization of agriculture	Decline in industrial employment in the core Decline of tertiary employment in the core Stabilization of employment in industry and tertiary sector in suburbs (ring) Decline of land prices in the city centre, spreading from there Growing employment in medium-sized agglomerations situated in the environment of the declining large functional urban regions (FURs)
Living	Heavy growth of cores due to immigration Construction of new residential quarters in the core: unity of living and working Expansion outside historical city-centre, rise of a national metropolis, or a dispersed system of equivalent cities, filling-up of municipal land area Underdevelopment of services	Migration from the country to the core as well as from the core to ring Construction of new residential areas at the core fringe and in suburban places, with segregation of living and working Qualitative improvement of city life via greenery, public utilities, amenities Expansion of municipal land area Start of reconstruction of historic town quarters Stronger suburbanization across larger area Slowing down of growth of larger cores	Growing population in medium-sized agglomerations Stagnating house building in suburban places Increased outmigration of households from core to ring and from city and suburbs to smaller agglomerations Decrease in immigration to agglomeration Decline of number of households in the agglomeration Decline in demand for high-quality housing Increasing number of housing units is demolished Population decline in suburban places; accelerated population decline in city
Traffic	Construction of transport system, esp. public transport; consequently expansion of core along and near transport lines Traffic connections between cores	Extension of traffic system Improvement of inner-city accessibility Quick expansion of car ownership Increasing mobility, esp. private transport Increasing traffic congestion and parking problems in the city	Declining use of public transport

TABLE 9.2.

Problems connected with spatial developments in stages of urbanization

	Urban development stages		
Problems in the sphere of	Urbanization	Suburbanization	Desurbanization and inter-urban decentralization
Working	Economic problems in agriculture redundant labour force and outmigration from rural areas Growth of the core amid stagnating environment Shortage of labour in the core Sub-optimum work conditions Increase of land prices in the core	Rise of tertiary sector instead of older forms of employment Threat to residential function of the city Decline of small-scale employment Decreased accessibility of the centre Loss of employment in the city Growing employment in suburban ring	Accelerated loss of employment in the core Decline in turnover for retailers; catering trade and other services in the core accelerate Increased non-used building capacity in offices
Living	Shortage of houses Construction of qualitatively bad houses High density of population Insufficient level of amenities Social and hygienic effects of unity of living and working Environmental pollution and lack of space Considerable differences in welfare level between urban and rural areas	Rising land prices in the city Loss of residential function in the core Segregation and ghetto forming of population groups Deterioration of historical parts of the core Slums in older core quarters, continuing reconstruction of the centre Monotony of life in suburban ring Administrative and financial problems Degradation of urban environment	Levelling off of urban hierarchy Increased segregation and ghetto forming of population groups Increased number of empty houses: open spots in city Increased criminality Losses in public utilities and amenities
Traffic	Insufficient transport capacity, particularly underdevelopment of urban transports in the major centres and its frequent absence in medium-sized and small towns	Traffic congestion in the centre due to increasing car density Insufficient capacity for journey-to-work traffic Parking problems and decreased accessibility of the centre Increasing need of transport and transport infrastructure Financial losses in public transport High external costs of traffic Increasing need for development of areas for weekend recreation	Increasing deficits in public transport Declining use of urban traffic facilities

TABLE 9.3.
Objectives of urban policy for stages of urbanization

	Urban development stages		
Objectives in the field of	Urbanization	Suburbanization	Desurbanization and inter-urban decentralization
Working	Economic growth via industrialization. concentrated in cores Development of tertiary employment in city centres Modernization of agriculture by land reallotments and mechanization Stabilization of rural labour force Betterment of working conditions	Spreading of employment to backward regions Abatement of regional differences Concentration of tertiary employment in modern city centres Improvement of social conditions in rural areas Only selective economic growth, constrained by social and environmental objectives	Reallocation of economic activities: f.i. offices out of city centre, creation of secondary centres of employment (multicentre city) Improvement of the employment situation Creation of new office locations in urban periphery Renewed integration of living and working within functional urban regions Limits to further tertiarization of city centres
Living	House construction for urban labour force Provision or urban amenities Improvement of urban quality of life Densification of housing by urban growth (flats, high buildings)	House construction for urban population in suburban areas, esp. private one-family houses Amenities within reasonable distance of residential quarters Modernization of city centres Decrease of house density Canalization of welfare levels in towns and between towns and rural areas Bundled deconcentration of people within functional urban region	Improvement of service sector in suburban places Stimulation of residential function of city centre Improving housing conditions for local population Maintenance of metropolitan functions Improving the supply of low-order facilities Limits to further decrease of house density in central city Improvement of urban quality of life
Traffic	Good urban transport system, esp. local public transport Creation of a motorway and railway network between urban centres Old city centres adapted to modern transportation requirements	Further construction of local public transport Better inter-urban transportation Infrastructure adapted to all needs of traffic: motorways, parkings, bridges, viaducts, etc. More integration of spatial consequences of traffic infrastructure More efficient use of existing transport facilities	Improvement of public transport facilities Restriction of long parking in city centre outside parking garages Creation of parking garages at accessible places Increasing city accessibility for public and private transport

TABLE 9.4.
Urban policy instruments for stages of urbanization

Instruments in the sphere of	Urban development stages		
	Urbanization	Suburbanization	Desurbanization and inter-urban decentralization
Working	Promotion of urban employment Compensation of costs of migration and removal Regional stimulation of depressed areas Agrarian reform of limited scope	Removal of manufacturing out of town Regional stimulation of depressed areas by means of investment premiums, migration arrangements, construction of social infrastructure, spreading of population in relation to concentration in urban areas Investment aid and state participation Spreading of governmental employment Strengthening of tertiary sector in towns Environmental protection laws, promotion of industrial research	Promotion of employment within an urban region Creation of new locations for industry and tertiary activities Clearance of old industrial locations by means of removal premiums, demolition of old infrastructure Active employment policy by means of location premiums, creation of necessary infrastructure
Living	Government aid for house construction Social housing act Qualitative improvement of urban environment: laying out of parks, green belts, garden cities, public services Corrections of urban boundaries Expansion of urban jurisdiction	City reconstruction: demolition of old living quarters and construction of new ones outside the town Measures to bundle suburbanization: new-town or growth-nuclei policy Promotion of a large-scale administrative structure for city and suburb Environmental protection, construction of accessible recreation areas Reorganization of urban-regional administration	Attraction of high-order facilities in suburbs, like hospitals, department stores, cultural amenities, etc. Creation of low-rent housing Restoring houses in use for offices to original residential destination Extension and creation of urban greenery where possible Increase in the police force Stimulation of housing in inner city by subsidies in land costs, restoration of old inner city parts
Traffic	Construction of traffic infrastructure, esp. public transport Nationalization of railway	Construction of a regional and national motorway system for the private motor-car Abatement of traffic congestion in and around cities by break-throughs for approaches, circle lines, parkings Subsidization of public transport Improving public transport in the city and to selected growth nuclei	Creation of pedestrian zones Improving parking facilities at walking distances More financial support by national government to support public transport in large functional urban regions

A question that merits obvious attention in an evaluation of the urban policies pursued in the countries participating in the present study is the extent to which those urban policies have been of an *ad-hoc* nature.

A policy aimed at the prevention of discrepancies is a different matter. According to strictly formal reasoning from the schemes presented such a policy will have to consider the problems that are inherent in the stage of development which is imminent. Looking to the future, the policy-maker will have to choose the tools which can help him reap the greatest possible net benefit. It may be expected that a government pursuing an integrated urban policy will contrive in advance to keep the negative effects of the next urbanization phase within reasonable bounds by using the instruments ranked one stage ahead in our schemes.

In principle, countries that have had the opportunity to acquaint themselves with the discrepancies between the actual and desirable urban living conditions prevailing in highly developed countries could turn that experience to advantage in formulating an adequate urban policy. Another aspect worth mentioning is that of the level of aspiration of certain countries at a given moment. Obviously, if a country raises its aspirations too high, the discrepancies in a development phase may be correspondingly grave.

9.3. Motives for urban policy

This section will deal in general terms with the question of the timing of a government's decision to pursue an explicit urban policy. The problem will first have to be presented in the most general context possible. To that end, a distinction between implicit and explicit policy will be introduced with respect to spatial policy, just as it was with respect to urban policy in Section 9.1. A government pursuing an explicit spatial policy will give priority to the realization of an explicitly desired spatial distribution of activities. Important features of an explicit spatial policy are, among others, a regional stimulation policy and a policy aimed at the deconcentration of activities in congestion areas. Stimulation policy is intended to accomplish a certain economic growth in selected regions; the purpose of a deconcentration policy is primarily to diminish the ill-effects of too much concentration of activities in congestion areas by spreading the activities. One of the instruments available to the government with which to realize the aims of regional stimulation and deconcentration policies is the promotion of spatial migration of capital and labour, a strategy that is commonly denoted as migration policy.

Now, as soon as a government makes explicit efforts, within the range of its regional-stimulation, deconcentration, or migration policy, to guide urban development either at a national or at a regional level, then it may be said that such a government is practising explicit urban planning.

In reality it appears that spatial and urban developments frequently proceed unplanned; in other words, the policy pursued frequently appears to have implicit urban aspects. What considerations may keep a government from explicitly introducing the spatial element into its policy?

First, it is not always recognized that the policy pursued has spatial aspects. In fact, any form of policy has by definition a spatial dimension. For any policy implies influencing the behaviour of individuals or groups of individuals, which is invariably manifested in space. Second, the spatial aspect of policy may be neglected because actual regional and urban developments correspond perfectly with those the government aspires to. In such a situation the spatial distribution of activities must allow optimum social welfare to be realized.

To appreciate how much the spatial and urban structure has contributed to social well-being, it is necessary to give concrete form to that well-being with the help of indicators selected for the purpose. The national income, employment, the impact on the environment, congestion phenomena, as well as their regional distribution can be used.

The choice of the indicators and the importance to be given to each component will depend on prevailing social preferences. If the confrontation of the actual spatial and urban structures with the desired situation represented by the preferences formulated does not lead to a policy aimed at the adjustment of those structures, one may conclude that the structures are not received as a social problem, or, to put it otherwise, that the social costs involved in an explicit adjustment of the spatial system are larger than the expected benefits.

However, with implicit urban policy it is often assumed in advance that the urban structure which finally emerges will contribute in the best way towards achieving the highest possible welfare level; afterwards it will become evident whether this optimism has been warranted or not.

When will the need for explicit urban policy arise? In general terms, that need will increase as the standard of urban development achieved is considered to be less than good, that is, when the national standard of welfare is lower than that which society considers to be within its reach. There are several reasons why spatial and urban structures are felt to be less than good and why they are therefore considered by a society as a separate determinant of social well-being. A process of national economic growth, for instance, may result in increased discrepancies between regions in terms of economic and urban development. Economic growth on the national level could result in growing discrepancies between the economic and urban development in individual regions, so much so that, even where social preferences remain unchanged, the conviction may be held that a more balanced spatial distribution of activities would positively affect national well-being. Both the benefits of economic growth—such as increased income, provisions, and employment—and its disadvantages—such as congestion, tension on the labour market, and loss of environmental quality—would then have to be spread equally. The government can endeavour, by means of explicit spatial policy, to direct the spread of activities in such a way as to create the spatial conditions for a maximum level of well-being. If, within such a policy, urban development is also planned explicitly, the government's policy is not only explicitly spatial but also explicitly urban in character. With the help of a policy a national government can influence in several ways the national urban-settlement pattern stimulating urban development in some places, checking or adjusting it elsewhere. When urban planning in a country consists of both types of measures, stimulation of urban development to promote economic growth, and deconcentration measures to counterbalance any negative external effects resulting from too much spatial concentration of activities, they should be coordinated as far as possible; only thus can the full social benefit be achieved.

From the foregoing the general conclusion may be drawn that explicit national urban planning will not be undertaken until the moment a government decides that it can raise national well-being through influencing the direction of national urban development. That moment arrives as soon as the actual national urban development has come to be considered a social problem.

10

Introduction to the Evaluation of National Urban Policies in Europe

Urban policy is partly an autonomous activity and partly a government's attempt to control certain undesirable growth tendencies and associated problems. These problems will not all have the same range. Some are of national or regional, others primarily of local import. In a country's urban policy it is therefore possible to distinguish a national, a regional, and a local urban policy. In each country the degree to which each administrative level is involved in urban policy depends on the one hand on the nature of the problems, and on the other hand on the distribution of responsibility and authority among the various levels of government. The centralization or decentralization of the political structure is reflected in this distribution.

Because of the format of the national reports of the CURB project,[1] attention will be given first and foremost to the urban policy pursued by national governments. Of course, in so doing it is not possible to gain a complete insight into the various ways in which public authorities deal with urban problems and try to influence the urban system at its various hierarchic levels. We want to examine how far national public authorities create frameworks within which urban developments can take place and which determine or regulate the local governments' policies.

Urban policy consists of all those measures that can influence the functioning of the urban system; the main components of that system which have been mentioned are employment, housing services, and transport. Furthermore, it has been pointed out that urban policy sense does not exist until an explicit urban dimension is added to general policy, i.e. until the

---

[1] To be published in Volume 2.

government conducts a policy that aims at achieving specific urban objectives such as the balanced spatial development of the main components mentioned above.

A distinction can be made in this connection between concentration areas and problem areas, the former being the most urbanized areas of a country, where most of the employment is concentrated, the latter the still predominantly agrarian areas, where employment and income are at a much lower level than in the concentration areas and urban areas which, because of their obsolete structure, are backward in comparison with the concentration areas. In many Western European countries, certain coal-mining districts and areas with a mostly obsolete industrial structure belong to the last-mentioned category.

The existence side-by-side of concentration and problem areas is an important factor in influencing a country's urbanization pattern. Push-and-pull factors cause a concentration area to work as an attraction pole to people and enterprises all over the country. Migration flows from the rural areas to the town maintain, and even reinforce, the concentration areas' strong position.

The growth of a concentration area passes through several stages. First, a town, surrounded by but still separated from stagnating rural areas, begins to expand. The economic base of such a town may be composed of mainly new industrial activities, trade activities, or administrative activities. Typically, there is rapid extension, exceeding the borders of the original town. Surrounding places are either absorbed at once in the town's built-up area or sucked into the town's sphere of influence. As growth continues, the area of expansion widens, and the suburbanization process draws the surrounding half-agrarian districts into the urban development.

So far, we have described the development of a separate town. It is typical of an urban concentration area that it does not comprise just one town, but is a conglomeration of large and small towns and associated places of all sizes with strong mutual ties. The centre of such an area may be an all-dominating metropolis like London, Paris, Vienna, Budapest, or Warsaw; it can also consist of a constellation of more or less equivalent towns; examples of such constellations are the urban concentration areas in Sweden, Germany, Belgium, and the Netherlands.

Urban concentration areas determine a country's urban development, because of their strong attraction. They tend to speed up the decline of peripheral areas or at any rate to delay their development, if no special measures are taken to keep the development of the different areas in a country in balance.

We have already mentioned stimulation and deconcentration as components of spatial policy. A policy of stimulation is geared explicitly to the needs of problem areas; though mostly a regional economic matter, it nearly always has implications for urban development in the regions concerned, and directly affects other regions. A policy of deconcentration, or spread, concerns both kinds of regions, because spread implies the movement from concentration areas to other areas. Frequently both kinds of policy run parallel: lack of space and the phenomena of congestion may call for the delay of further growth in concentration areas, thereby opening new prospects for stimulating problem areas.

In the following chapters separate attention will be paid to urban policy in relation to core regions as well as to problem regions. Special attention will also be paid to the nature of planning.

11

Urban Policy in Relation to Core Regions

11.1. Introduction

In this chapter the policy in relation to urbanized concentration areas is the subject for discussion. Attention will be focused on urban-organization policy and on that aspect of deconcentration policy that is supposed to solve problems in concentration areas. In previous chapters the evolution of urban areas has been divided into several stages as in a life-cycle. Like a living organism, a town starts its existence at a low level. If conditions are favourable, a period of growth follows, growth that may be rapid or gradual, as circumstances permit. A town's growth is attended by physical expansion beyond its original borders. As the town goes on growing and expanding, there may become a moment in its life-cycle when certain parts of the urban area, for instance the centre, begins to be seriously congested. Congestion means that the existing spatial structure is no longer adequate to accommodate all the activities that are essential to the town's functioning. For the urban system to survive it then becomes necessary that the spatial structure is renovated, and a planning policy instigated.

Roughly speaking, we distinguished three stages in urban development: one of urbanization, that is, growth, one of suburbanization involving mainly deconcentration of growth, and one of desurbanization.

A few preliminary points must be made.

First, the various stages are not clear cut. Frequently the transition from one urbanization stage to another is difficult to pinpoint. Urbanization should be looked upon as a continuous revolutionary process, one phase passing gradually to the next.

This is equally true of a society's development from an agrarian economy to a tertiary one, where most of the employment is located within the

124

service sectors. There, too, dividing lines must be considered mere indications of the periods during which a society is structurally altered.

Second, it must not be forgotten that the regions within a country may well show wide differences in economic development. The larger a country, the greater the differences may be. A relatively small country like the Netherlands will have regional differences in economic development that are of a lesser nature than those in a relatively large country like Italy. Accordingly, regions within a country may be in quite different stages of urbanization; it will then be necessary to regionalize the urbanization phasing in that country (see Chapter 6).

In the following sections we shall analyse policy measures aimed at specific urbanization stages distinguished as far as they have been discussed in the national reports. The analysis will be limited to a number of typical problem areas; no attempt will be made to present an overall picture.

11.2. Urban policy in the urbanization phase

In the early stages of the urban-growth process, the urbanization means primarily migration from rural areas to developing towns, some typical policy problems occur. In the period under observation in this project, that of the years after the Second World War, many European countries changed from a rural agrarian society to an industrial society, notably the Eastern European countries Poland, Bulgaria, Hungary, and Yugoslavia, and, to some extent, Italy and France. The measures required are partly the same as those taken by countries faced with the task of rebuilding cities that were destroyed in the war. The difference between the two categories of countries lies in the cause of the urban-growth process. In the four Eastern European countries mentioned it was the result of the switch from an agrarian to an industrial economy which encouraged a strong flow of people to the towns. In countries like Germany, Belgium, the Netherlands, and, again to some extent, France and Italy, urbanization was well under way before 1940. These countries had to rebuild their towns for people who had lived in them for some time. Rebuilding, however, paved the way for further urbanization.

In the four Eastern European countries a purposeful industrialization policy laid the basis for urbanization. Hitherto the countries concerned had been mainly agrarian practising a labour-intensive type of agriculture. The income level was low and employment prospects for the agrarian population slender. The social structure of the rural districts tended to perpetuate the situation. After the war, with its drastic political changes, the new authorities gave full priority to the social and economic progress of the people, and the strategy chosen was that of accelerated industrialization, and rationalization of agriculture.

Industrialization implies a change in the proportions of the urban and rural population. Industrialization leads to a concentration of people, and hence to urbanization. In the countries under observation the effect was more marked as the emphasis was laid on heavy industry, and on large-scale production which would benefit from the economies of scale. Large plants with thousands of workers had to be located where there were masses of people, to find an adequate labour supply. Once they were there, these plants attracted many more people to the town.

The production techniques applied also encouraged urbanization; the work was done with a relatively large labour force and few machines. In addition to the tendency to locate large-scale, labour-intensive industries near large towns, some economic considerations can be identified that were of fundamental importance to urban policy. In the building and modernization of their countries, socialist governments were faced with a great scarcity of capital. The main problem was how to spend the available capital as efficiently as possible, given the social objectives and priorities. The policy decided upon was first of all to give the country a sound basis to ensure its prosperity. Efficient use of capital, that is maximum production with a given amount of capital, or attaining a production target at minimum cost, implied the allocation of financial means to large-scale projects in towns, for thus economies of scale could be achieved, and the infrastructure already present in the town utilized, for as long as its capacity was not exceeded.

It should be pointed out, however, that the availability of an ample supply of labour is in most cases a necessary but not sufficient condition for a region or state to qualify for the settlement of new industries in the framework of an industrialization policy. Because heavy basis industries were the government's first industrialization choice, their location was also determined by the availability of cheap inputs, such as raw and ancillary materials.

So, the first areas to be industrialized were those richly endowed with raw materials—coal, ores, etc.—and places where raw materials arrived, such as the area around seaports. It was indeed these two types of regions that showed strong economic and urban growth.

Industrialization as a means of economic growth tends to increase the differences in economic and urban development between regions, because regions differ in their access to relevant location factors. Indeed, a government will have to decide whether it will follow a strategy promising maximum growth of the national product, accepting the resultant regional differences in economic development, or a strategy likely to encourage a balanced development of the regions, accepting a more restricted growth of the national income.

It is clear that the countries which entered the urbanization stage after the war, among them the four Eastern European countries mentioned above, chose to allocate industries in such a way as to maximize the growth of the national income.

It was, indeed, a policy favouring national economic efficiency. In Section 11.3 the degree to which the spatial spread of activities was an explicit object of policy and the timing of that policy will be investigated; the role of urban planning will be given special attention.

From their national reports[1] it appears that governments have not always succeeded in controlling and compensating for the side effects of industrialization. Conditions in rural areas dropped further and further behind, while the pressure of migrants on the town increased; in some cases rural areas were seriously depopulated. Not only regional development, but also social and urban planning were less than optimum. While industrialization was given top priority, too few resources could be allocated to housing, services, and consumption goods. A tremendous housing shortage in the towns is a typical feature of this period. In most countries the first houses built were of poor quality, and little was done to improve their environment. Improvements had to wait until an increased production capacity brought about greater prosperity. In Poland, Hungary, and Bulgaria the turning-point came in the middle of the 1960s; from then on the economic policy had no longer top priority: attention began to be given to social objectives. Housing and provisions (shops, community centres, facilities for sport and recreation, public transport) came high on the priority list. In Poland, plans for town extensions are based on a division of the area into monofunctional units, i.e. on the separation of residential and working areas. Residential areas are built up of units: "districts" of apartment buildings, with provisions allocated according to a hierarchic pattern. Green belts and recreation facilities are laid out around these districts, always according to the accepted standards of the moment. In plans for work areas, protection against environmental pollution and the efficient use of infrastructure are beginning to be considered. The expansion of towns and urban regions had to be adapted to suit the local transport system (trams, buses, underground railway). A certain measure of deconcentration is being attempted. There are bottlenecks, mostly the result of a relative shortage of resources. We have seen how, under the pressure of housing shortages and the rapid growth of towns, new housing quarters, provided with only the barest essentials, had to be constructed in

[1] See Volume 2.

a very short time. Sometimes these quarters are too far from the town centre, because it is as yet impossible to replace old houses nearer the centre with new ones. The extensions resulted mostly from the postponement of reconstruction in the inner city, for both economic and technical reasons; a greater number of housing units can be built rapidly in the peripheries of the city. The maintenance of existing dwellings has often been neglected.

Policy-makers have tried to remove the bottlenecks in various ways. First, by trying to check the growth of the largest towns, spreading urbanization over a number of centres all over the country. Second, by a progressive policy of urban (re-)planning and town renovation. Both aspects will be dealt with more fully in Sections 11.4 and 11.5 respectively.

In general it may be said that the problems of urbanization may give rise to a change in policy, in the sense that governments will start giving more attention than before to the urban implications of their actions. Policies will be followed which contribute as much as possible to that form of urbanization which seems most desirable from a social point of view. Thus, in the course of the urbanization phase, urban planning may pass from being implicit to being explicit. In this context, the idea of a national urbanization pattern may be born, and for the first time an attempt may be made to give explicit substance to a desirable nationwide urban development scheme.

11.3. Towards a national plan for urban development

Ideas about a national urbanization pattern do not emerge until a certain degree of urbanization has been reached and the various towns in a country are seen to belong to a national system. The concept of a system implies that its parts are interrelated and the development in one place affects what happens elsewhere.

Rarely is urban growth distributed quite evenly across a whole country. Owing to historical, geographical, or economic factors, one area offers better prospects for development than another. Consequently, without intervention or regulation urban growth will be limited to just a few places, while other areas lag behind in employment, income, or level of provisions.

Urban planning on a national scale aims at promoting further urbanization where the net results are in the best interest of the country as a whole, given the space available and generally accepted socio-economic objectives. In theory, the corresponding policy may favour anything from a high degree of concentration to maximum deconcentration. In practice, however, we mainly observe policies oriented towards polycentric development.

The philosophy behind such policies is that towns form a hierarchy, that is, are on higher or lower levels in relation to one another. In an agrarian region, a certain location pattern of settlements can be recognized. At the top of the hierarchy, and centrally situated, is the regional centre. Around it there are centres of a lower order which are smaller in size, and around each of them still smaller centres, ranking lower in the hierarchy. Ideally, a hexagonal location pattern emerges. The geographic implications of the hierarchy concept have now been dropped almost completely. What is left is the functional meaning: settlements have a certain relationship with one another, one functioning as a centre of a higher order than the others. The highest-order function of a centre is based on its size and its amenities. Amenities in the fields of education, culture, research, and technology tend to be so large that they can only successfully be located in a large town. In lower-order centres amenities catering for a smaller area are found. The lowest level consists of small rural villages, which can only cater for some of the daily and most frequently occurring needs of the people living in and around them.

In accordance with the notion of a hierarchic structure, many countries operate a division into primary, secondary, and tertiary centres, or into national, regional, and local centres. The implication of the hierarchy concept for the national urbanization pattern is that it provides an argument for an even spread of towns across the country and in particular for the stimulation of secondary towns next to already existing large towns at a national level, including the national capital. The notion of hierarchical structure and diffusion has strongly influenced regional employment policies. Government measures have been oriented towards those towns that clearly could fulfil a function in the national urban system. The hierarchy concept also linked urban policy with regional policy, which had come to be governed by a similar concept: the growth pole theory.

An urban policy along hierarchy lines is being pursued in many European countries, notably Austria, Belgium, Bulgaria, France, Hungary, Switzerland, and Yugoslavia.

Traditional thinking in terms of an urban hierarchy is based on the idea of separate, autonomous towns. There are countries, however, where several towns together have grown into conglomerations, within which the relationships are different from those within an urban system of individual towns.

The use of the expression "functional urban region" is characteristic of this transition. An urban region extends over a wider area than a town, and within it certain parts are set aside for specific functions: work area, residential area, shopping area, main centre, sub-centre, etc. The simplest pattern of such a FUR is that of a central town surrounded by a ring of sub-centres oriented to that central town. Another pattern is that of several equivalent centres each with its sub-centres. In many European countries such urban regions lie so near together that urban units of a higher rank are formed, denoted by such terms as urban zone, conglomeration, or metropolitan area. Examples of these are South Sweden, South-east England, the Rimcity in the western part of the Netherlands, the Ruhr Area in Western Germany, the Antwerp–Brussels axis in Belgium, and the regions around the gigantic cities of Paris, London, Vienna, Warsaw, and Budapest. In Poland a similar form of urbanization exists in the south, in the industrial area of Silesia.

Where such conglomerations exist, urban policy will have to be based on principles different from those applicable to traditional hierarchies. The organization of such extensive urban areas, and the delimitation of town and country, now become the main problems. When urbanization has advanced thus far, the need to preserve and protect the few remaining rural areas against what is called "urban sprawl" becomes generally felt, and urban policy will be formulated accordingly. Indeed, in the national reports from Great Britain, France, the Netherlands, and Poland the national urbanization pattern is evidently conceived of in terms of containment policies to restrict further growth of the largest towns and unregulated suburbanization.

11.4. Growth limitation and suburbanization

Many countries have taken measures to limit the further growth of their largest towns and to regulate progressive decentralization. There are three situations in which the former becomes imperative.

1. After a period of rapid expansion in population and employment. If the existing provisions prove inadequate for the influx of people, and have not kept pace with the growth of the population, further growth may entail serious congestion and a shortage of houses, schools, public services, health care, recreation, and public transport. Not only will it be possible to provide adequate accommodation for new inhabitants of the town, the position of people already living there will also get relatively worse. A provisional check on growth is then indicated until the level of facilities has caught up with the needs of the population. In most cases such discrepancies are due to a one-sided policy aimed only at economic objectives to the detriment of social objectives.

2. When the growth of towns is attended by serious delays in the development of areas elsewhere in the country.

As soon as the national development policy is no longer oriented exclusively towards maximum economic growth, but aspires towards an acceptable distribution of growth across the whole country, there is an argument for redirecting resources away from the (big) towns to less strong backward areas. Such a policy has been characterized as a dispersal policy. It usually runs parallel with the stimulation problem areas. Relevant measures are concerned first and foremost with the creation of employment, or with the creation—for example with the help of infrastructural or regional welfare policy—of conditions that may be conducive to the expansion of employment.

3. When a town has either exhausted its geographical possibilities for its expansion or, according to the "threshold theory", has reached the point where the costs of further growth would be greater than those of expanding lesser towns. This theory assumes that there is a relationship between a town's population and the costs associated with its function, and that beyond a certain optimum size the costs will increase more than is proportionate to the population growth, owing to the complex infrastructure required, the strain on public resources, the rise of land prices due to increased demand, and in general, to congestion in the flow of people, goods, and communication systems.

These three situations may occur singly or in combination; the control of growth based on considerations under (2) and (3) can notably be combined with those of regional policy.

A meaningful distinction can be made in this connection between the original central town and the total urban area, consisting of the centre and its dependent surrounding areas. Measures to check further growth may concern only the central city, or the total FUR, or even only the (suburban) ring round the central city. Measures taken in one area usually have repercussions in another. Later on in this report it will be shown that suburbanization is to a great extent an answer to the lack or the limitation of growth prospects in the town itself.

Specific urban policy

So far we have talked about growth-checking measures in a general sense. In more concrete terms such measures apply to employment, housing, or transport. It is common practice to make a distinction between measures which directly limit further growth, particularly prohibition measures, and measures that do so indirectly, e.g. via the price mechanism.

With regard to employment, we speak of direct growth-checking measures when a national or local public authority forbids any increase in the number of jobs. In centrally directed economies, where most people are employed in state industries, such prohibitions are the easiest to enforce. Planning authorities there have relatively more direct power to create new employment elsewhere or to move existing industries. In economies that are not centrally directed, governments only have power over that sector of employment for which they are themselves responsible. Private enterprises are essentially free to locate where they find the most advantageous conditions. By using legal measures a government can intervene in private location behaviour. Some of these have a direct character; they are prohibitive measures. Among them are licensing systems for new investment in industry or in the service sector. A licence may refer to location or expansion in general, but also to a certain aspect of location, such as environmental damage (air or water pollution or noise nuisance); in the latter case the regulations can be so strict as to prevent establishment. Examples can be found in all the Western European national studies. England has the longest tradition in this matter, where immediately after the Second World War the Industrial Development Certificate system was introduced, to be followed later (in 1964) by a similar system for the location of offices and services. In France, a similar system has been introduced for the Paris area.

The government has direct responsibility for those employed in its own administrative offices. In some countries, e.g. England and the Netherlands, the government has undertaken to move a part of its administration offices elsewhere, to relieve the capital as well as to stimulate peripheral regions. These tend to be sited a long way from the capital in towns in declining regions rather than in satellite or new towns within the capital's sphere of influence. In this practice England and the Netherlands took such initiatives.

Sometimes the policy of spreading government services was extended to office locations in general. In the Netherlands, for instance, some municipal authorities issued strict rules limiting further extension of offices in inner cities, to prevent other concerns from being ousted and to relieve the congestion, which may be partly ascribed to a surfeit of offices.

Besides direct measures, indirect measures can help to control the development of employment in large towns. Most of them, working through the price mechanism, tend to make location in towns relatively more expensive, or location elsewhere relatively cheaper. One effective means to this end is a system of levies on new investments in the urban area set against a system of premiums and subsidies or tax facilities on investments elsewhere. Another important factor is the interest rate for loans granted by the government, which can be differentiated according to the area of location or expansion. This method is used both in Eastern and in Western Europe; although in Western Europe the interest rate itself is not controlled, the credit guarantees are used differentially.

Other indirect measures aim at creating attractive conditions for investment in places where they are wanted, for the construction of roads, industrial sites, schools, residential facilities, etc. Such measures are traditionally a part of the regional stimulation policy, and will be included in the discussion of that policy. The aim is at enabling a less attractive site to compete with the stronger urban concentration areas.

Besides employment, housing construction offers the government another opportunity to control the growth of towns. Again a distinction can be made between direct and indirect government responsibility: the government has more or less direct responsibility for regulating house building. The effectiveness of their measures depends on what happens in other fields of government policy, particularly in the field of employment development. Economic and social objectives should at least be adjusted to each other. The countries studied offer examples of friction in that area, for instance when control of the growth of the largest towns is advocated while the location of industries in the urban area is uncontrolled. If the controlling measures only affect the provision of houses and other facilities or transport infrastructure, discrepancies are bound to occur, discrepancies that express themselves in deteriorating living conditions for the growing population, extension of the urban area in places where houses can still be built, e.g. in the suburban ring, and more commuting and worse traffic problems. On the other hand, the various countries give instances where plans for spreading employment to stimulation areas were not attended by adequate measures to adjust the residential areas and the level of provisions in those areas. As a result the desired "spreading" either has not succeeded for lack of incentives, or has given rise to new problems besetting housing and living conditions in stimulation areas.

Common measures used are: control of immigration through a system of housing licences, sometimes combined with work licences regulating of building either directly through building licences, or indirectly through price measures in the shape of differentiated land prices or taxes on real estate.

A major aspect of the measures aimed at limiting house building in urban areas is the spatial differentiation within that urban area. Limitation of further growth often affects only the city centre, either because the town has been built up entirely, or because the government wants to reserve some space there for new economic provisions belonging to the centre. In that case policy may be directed towards promoting or permitting suburbanization, or towards the formation of "new towns". A new-town policy is a proper decentralization policy as far as urban development is concerned, while suburbanization is rather an autonomous and uncontrolled process.

Suburbanization, as we see it here, is the result of push as well as pull factors. On the one hand, it is an answer to a lack of housing facilities in the town, or to their decline as a result of a change in the town's functions, causing residential areas in and around the centre to give way to industries and infrastructure. As a consequence, town dwellers are forced to escape to the outskirts, or to surrounding places where houses can still be made available, and migrants from rural areas to the town do not get beyond suburban places. There are other factors that encourage suburbanization. Living conditions outside the centre may be considered more attractive because the population diversity is lower, there is the chance of owning a house of one's own, the natural environment is better, etc. Rising prosperity, and greater mobility, make a move out of town possible; it is first and foremost the well-to-do that can afford to live outside the town, commuting daily to their jobs and the central amenities of the city.

Without discussing in detail all aspects of suburbanization, we would point out two facts that are of particular importance in urban policy.

First: if urban growth proceeds according to the suburbanization model, the urban area will be inclined to extend without a proper structure, and the adequate functioning of all the parts of the urban system can only be ensured at extremely high costs. Such a growth pattern is neatly described by the term "urban sprawl": the town falls apart in a larger number of little units, each of them too small to benefit from the agglomeration advantages inherent in urban concentration.

Second: because urban sprawl is selective in favour of the high-income groups, the city centre threatens to become a social ghetto for the less well endowed, and the replacement of too many houses by industries, particularly by offices, can lead to congestion. The interaction between the two processes—ghetto-building and congestion—is detrimental to the town's survival as the multifunctional centre of an urban district. Congestion and impoverization also threaten employment prospects and the amenities in the town. In a number of countries the government tries to solve the problems by town renovation; a separate section will be devoted to this. The response of policy-makers to urban sprawl will be an attempt to keep inevitable decentralization under control by planning it according to the principle of "polycentric development". This principle is given its most positive form in the "new-town policy". The idea is that when decentralization of a town becomes necessary because of progressive growth or because functional changes in the town cause an outflow of citizens, the decentralization process should be guided towards selected places at some distance from the original town. In these places enough people should be concentrated for new towns to be formed and for urban sprawl to be brought to a halt. The basis of the new towns should be broad enough to cater for public and commercial establishments. Infrastructure can only be built profitably if there are enough to use it.

In new-town policy, the geographic scale determines whether the aim is primarily to establish satellite towns around the original central town, or to build entirely new, independent towns. Satellite towns provide housing and associated services, but are tied to the central town as far as employment is concerned. Such a form of concentrated decentralization eliminates certain disadvantages of urban sprawl, but at the same time tends to increase commuting and for that reason is no great help in preventing traffic congestion in the urban area. The urban area is simply extended, albeit in a structured pattern of main core and reasonably large sub-cores.

New-town policy can also aim to create entirely new, independent towns, whose inhabitants no longer depend on the original urban concentration area, not even for their employment. To that effect, jobs need to be moved with the population, so that the new town becomes a full-grown working and living area. Such new towns appear much more difficult to realize in practice, especially if the government has no direct authority over the location behaviour of (private) industries. In that case, methods used to encourage businesses to move are indirect ones; they can do no more than create conditions that make moving attractive. New-town policy in the latter sense is really regional policy, aiming at the stimulation of a region by creating an urban centre. At this point, urban policy and regional policy coincide.

The two kinds of new-town policy can be observed in the countries studied. In England, the first country to introduce a new-town policy, the towns were at first built only a relatively short distance from London. It is no wonder therefore that they partly developed into satellite towns that became fully integrated into the urban system of London and South-east England. Not until later was new-town policy used to stimulate backward regions at a greater distance from London. The major methods for getting employment moved to these areas were, as mentioned earlier, limiting measures in London itself, moving state services, and stimulating regional development.

In France two policies have been pursued simultaneously: the "villes nouvelles" policy around Paris and the "métropoles d'équilibre" policy elsewhere.

In Poland a policy has been conducted for some time which aims to establish some twenty urban agglomerations across the whole country. Within the agglomerations, new towns in the limited sense of satellite towns are being founded.

In the Netherlands so far a new-town policy has been pursued in the limited sense of promoting concentrated residential units around the existing large towns, this being known as growth-core policy. Only since the

1970s has there been a spread of urbanization to parts of the country outside the Randstad in the west.

The examples given may be found in other countries also. They give rise to a few concluding remarks.

The original new-town policy has evolved in two directions. On the one hand it seeks to fight the worst drawbacks of suburbanization by arranging people and activities in a pattern around a town. Such a policy helps to solve problems in the central town by creating residences for people who (must) leave the town, and it contributes to the structured urbanization of the surrounding countryside, making it possible also to realize objectives regarding the preservation of environment, public transport, local level of amenities, etc. The scale on which the policy works is that of the region; it contributes only in an indirect way to a national urbanization pattern.

On the other hand, new-town policy has become a matter of regional policy as well as an element of a national urbanization policy. The original new-town concept is lost almost entirely in this case. The aim is no longer the founding of new towns, but the stimulation of new urban growth in existing towns to stimulate regional growth. This form of policy primarily requires the dispersal of jobs towards the new urban areas, commuting being out of the question because of the longer distances involved. Here there is less chance of success, because it is more difficult to spread employment over long distances than to move residences within the urban district. The effectiveness of a dispersing and stimulation policy will be discussed later. In formulating a national settlement strategy, i.e. to plan and control urbanization in the whole country, this form of new-town policy is essential.

Along with housing and jobs, transport can be mentioned as a separate sector to which measures restricting urban growth in concentration areas can be applied. It is not really correct to treat transport as a separate sector, however, as it is indeed a derivative of the former two. The demand for a transport system depends on work and residential areas.

The fact that transport is nevertheless dealt with here as a separate component is due to the wide influence of measures that affect transport and to the fact that urban problems are so often transport problems. The importance of transport in spatial development is apparent from a few examples. Regional stimulation and the promotion of urban development in underdeveloped areas start with opening up that region to transport systems, through the construction of roads and other infrastructure. The functioning of an urban centre in relation to the whole agglomeration depends on the accessibility of the centre. Large-scale suburbanization cannot be accomplished without good transport connections between rural areas and the town. A town's pressure on a rural area increases as connections with the regional transport network improve.

Even when measures concerning transport are not taken for the express purpose of influencing urban development, they will still have that effect. In our terminology such measures are the results of implicit urban policy.

If the government's objective is to check or at any rate regulate urban growth, the measures taken will often be of a negative nature, consisting, for instance, in leaving certain elements of infrastructure unbuilt. We can distinguish in this connection regional and local measures.

Regulating the suburbanization process according to the principles of patterned deconcentration implies supplying infrastructure only where it is desirable, that is by connecting with the centre those places that have been selected as "growth cores". Where traffic congestion is a problem too, it is important to allow for the right mixture of public and private transport. The advantage of a new-town policy over urban sprawl is that the new towns are large enough to warrant the construction and exploitation of public transport systems.

If suburbanization within urban concentration areas is kept in check according to a policy of spreading activities to problem areas and stimulating development there, it is imperative to provide such areas with adequate transport facilities. In many countries a national road network has been constructed or extended in keeping with regional and urban policy. Local traffic and transport policy should be in harmony with the regional and national policies. Coordination and harmonization between the various levels of public authority as far as transport policy is concerned is evidently one of the most difficult problems. In the present context, the first task of local policy-makers as far as traffic is concerned is to solve the congestion resulting from urban growth and mass car ownership. Congestion is to a considerable extent due to the specific spatial shape of many of our towns and the high concentration of employment in the central business district. Moreover, it is there that important central provisions of an administrative, cultural, educational, and commercial nature are concentrated. Around it, extending outward to the ring of spacious suburbs, lie the residential quarters. The result is a large traffic flow to and from the centre, especially at peak hours. To solve the resulting traffic problems it is essential that residential and working areas are located in a more balanced way, so that there is less traffic and the road capacity is better used. Of course, measures to achieve such a balance fall outside the scope of transport policy; they belong to spatial policy. The association made here proves once more how essential an integrated spatial policy is. Because it is not possible to divert all traffic flows, measures of traffic policy may still be necessary. Two types of measures suggest themselves. First, those that aim at upgrading the urban road network so as to improve accessibility and encourage smooth traffic flow. For that purpose ring roads have been constructed in many towns, and new roads have been cut through the town. Second, attempts to fight congestion and parking problems in the centre by encouraging public transport to take over a greater proportion of urban traffic. To that effect, underground railway systems have been and are being built, tram and bus services promoted, and, in addition, measures restricting parking in the centre introduced.

In most cases a traffic policy seems to come after events instead of preceding them. It tries to adjust to traffic needs as they are, rather than to influence traffic-generating factors to such an extent that traffic develops in harmony with other objectives of urban policy.

11.5. Town reconstruction and town renovation

In previous sections of this chapter a number of aspects of urban development and associated urban policies have been discussed. Specific topics included the urbanization policy in Eastern European countries, and the policy pursued in all countries to build up a national settlement system. Measures taken to realize the desired urban system were found to be taken at a national and regional level on the one hand, and a local level on the other. At a national level there were measures to limit growth and spread the population and activities from congested areas, and to stimulate urbanization in peripheral regions. In that context, a policy of suburbanization was discussed. The relevant national policy must be implemented at a local level. But in order to realize a desired urban system local measures are also needed that spring not from dispersal or stimulation motives, but from the development and organization of the urban area as such. One aspect we want to deal with is that of town reconstruction and town renovation.

The shaping and renovation of an urban structure is a continuous process affecting the whole lifetime of a town. However, in most European towns the period just after the war represented a new departure: they found themselves faced with the task of rebuilding all that had been destroyed in the war. That period, however interesting and significant for later developments, is not the one that concerns us. We want to focus attention on policies that try to deal with what has come to be referred to as the urban crisis. This crisis is mainly brought about by progressive decentralization, which threatens to make the town's centre lose its original role as the academic and cultural heart of a large urban district. The symptoms of the crisis are a rapidly declining population, bad living conditions, traffic congestion, environmental pollution, and declining employment as industries start to follow the population's outward move. The point has been reached where, in some countries, the problem areas are considered to be no longer the traditional stimulation areas, but the large towns (see Part II).

The question is whether this evolution is inevitable, the result of an autonomous process, or if the government has the power to reverse the trend and offer a new lease of life to inner cities. The problem is most urgent in some Western European cities and is related to the present state of their socio-economic development, of which we have described the characteristics earlier.

Many of the cities involved, although not all, come into being, as far as their present layout is concerned, during a period of industrialization, in most cases in the nineteenth century and the beginning of the twentieth. The spatial layout still has the features of that time. A large portion of the built-up area in the town centre and of the street network is still on a nineteenth-century scale. In the meantime the economic structure has changed.

Modern large-scale industries, involving advanced technology, were the first to move to the outskirts, where in most cases they were concentrated on specific industrial sites. The spaces in the centre that fell vacant were filled, sometimes by houses, but more often by new forms of tertiary services. Tall office buildings were erected, mostly belonging to the business sector: banks, insurance companies, press offices, and government buildings. To make centres of employment accessible, new transport systems had to be constructed in the shape of roads, railways, some of them underground. The introduction and mass production of the private car has greatly increased the need for such provisions. The centres of many (Western) European towns continued to be flooded with offices, thereby losing their residential function. Old residential quarters had to give way to the pressure of town reconstruction. Time and again the nineteenth-century spatial structure failed to accommodate the exigencies of the twentieth century. Towns that were utterly destroyed and had to be rebuilt after 1945 have some advantages over others, but in 1945 the drastic changes that were to come about from 1960 onwards could not be foreseen. An old town is in a serious predicament in this era of motor cars. The population leaves for suburbia, provisions directly associated with it follow suit, services in the tertiary sector, greatly impeded by the increasing congestion, sometimes decide to move out too, the financing of urban amenities is in jeopardy because the local government's income is as a rule closely related to the number of inhabitants. The population dwindles as do financial resources, but the urban facilities are still used as intensively by the people living in the suburbs and by the industries in the town.

In this situation those responsible for urban policy are confronted with two possible courses of action.

First, a municipal government may pursue a policy of town reconstruction, by which we understand a policy that is essentially adjusted to the prevailing trends, and, accepting the present division of roles between centre and suburbs, sets out to eliminate the bottlenecks as much as possible. As far as living is concerned that implies that the suburbanization process is brought under control, so that new satellite towns or growth cores are founded which can be linked with the town centre in a responsible way with the help of infrastructure. Traffic is carefully and cautiously regulated, but no attempt is made to discourage employment in the city centre. Accessibility is improved by measures making for a smooth and fast flow of traffic through the town, and for neat solutions to parking problems. As a residential quarter, the centre is discarded; it will henceforth serve as a centre of tertiary employment and as a refined shopping centre, certainly not for daily necessities.

The second approach open to a municipality is entirely different: that of town renovation. By town renovation we understand here an effort to restore to a town its former broad function. The first priority is to make people return to the town to live, or at least to stop the rapid depopulation.

In regional as in urban policy, a shift in priorities can be observed. At first, regional problems, particularly that of unemployment, were solved by creating jobs in towns and thus encouraging people to migrate from country to town. When migration had proceeded to the point where the rural areas threatened to be depopulated, regional policy switched to the principle of "taking the work to the people". For a long time there has been a tendency in towns to improve living and working conditions by progressive decentralization. Then there came a moment when the disadvantages of such a policy for the town itself became manifest. Urban policy then tends to change from the first to the second mentioned approach. In the Netherlands and in Great Britain, for instance, the priority switch is very clear.

12

Urban Policy in Problem Areas

12.1. General remarks

In various countries, the unequal spatial distribution of urban growth across the national territory has led first to theories and then to policies concerning the most desirable national urban system. As a reaction to the actual situation, the policies tended towards a deconcentration of urban development. In general, the wish to a more polycentric development was found to be inspired by two main motives, the first being to fight the serious negative effects of spatial concentration that may occur in the so-called congested areas; limiting the growth in such areas is one of the remedies. The second is to stimulate the regions that in socio-economic terms lag behind the concentration areas; urbanization in the weak regions, to a degree that depends on the strategy adopted, is implied in the stimulation.

The two motives are not independent of each other, as may be seen when deconcentration is used as a means for regional stimulation. For instance, business enterprises that are dispersed to relieve concentration areas can be moved to centres in backward regions. Thus, both the development of a polycentric urban system and the stimulation of backward regions are achieved. From the point of view of urban policy it is vital that regional policy stimulates urbanization in regions specifically selected for the purpose. If urbanization is effected so as to make economic growth possible in those regions, we have to do with a form of regional policy of which urban planning constitutes an explicit element. Of course there are many forms of regional policy in which urban elements are only implicitly included; frequently such forms are the predecessors of explicit urban planning within a regional policy.

141

In this chapter attention is given to the ways in which the relationship between urban policy and regional policy has developed where the stimulation of economically weak problem areas in the different countries is concerned.

12.2. Migration policy

Migration policy represents one of the strategies that can be followed within a spatial policy. In principle, migration may refer to people as well as industries or capital goods. In this section we are concerned exclusively with migration policy in relation to people, and more specifically with their moves to and from problem regions and core regions according to the distinction adopted in this report. Given the theme of the present chapter, the emphasis is on the migration of people from problem areas to economically stronger areas. The relevant policy may be inspired by needs and requirements in either type of area. We shall examine the extent to which migration policy represents implicit or explicit urban policy.

When a government decides to stimulate migration from a problem area, the underlying consideration may be that there are as yet few prospects for building up the economy in that area itself. Even if the purpose of the policy is to fight unemployment and solve the associated problems in the problem region, migration to stronger regions may be the means chosen, because the region is not yet ripe for local development. The developmental maturity of a region is determined by the presence of the principal location requirements of commercial enterprises, such as accessible sales markets, sufficient labour, raw materials and ancillaries, technical and social infrastructure, and the advantages of an urban agglomeration.

If a region is not ripe for development, the funds available for stimulation would give too low a return when spent there instead of elsewhere. For that reason it may be advisable for a government to stimulate migration of people out of such an area, thus diminishing its socio-economic problems. That kind of policy mostly aims at influencing migration decisions by removing financial or psychological barriers by means of migration premiums, reimbursement of the cost of moving house, assistance in finding a new place to live, information about the new residential town, and so on.

In the longer run the general mobility of the population is increased effectively by means of education and training, thereby enabling people to respond more readily to prosperity differences at alternative locations with a decision to migrate.

In several European countries migration policies as described have greatly contributed to the solution of the socio-economic problems of the population in backward areas. Sweden is a striking example of a country where priority has been given to "taking the men to the jobs". In other countries a similar policy has been pursued; in the Netherlands it was applied in the period 1950–1965.

Migration policies as described above have had implications for urban development, though their main objective was to lessen economic problems and improve national income distribution. Employment and income security were found in economically stronger areas where the urban evolution was already well under way. By stimulating migration to concentration areas, migration policy has unintentionally contributed to the growth of urban areas; it was a policy with an implicit urban character. On the one hand, it stimulated the expansion of developed urban areas; on the other hand, it has had a negative effect on potential urban growth prospects in the problem areas. Although lessening unemployment and raising income, this form of migration policy has, in fact, increased the imbalance in the spatial distribution of urban cores.

It should be observed that the same type of policy has been pursued for quite different economic motives, viz. to promote the free flow of labour to those urban centres with greater possibilities of economic development than other areas. Migration policy in that sense was often an aid to industrialization. From an urbanization point of view, the effects were again implicit.

Unbridled urban development can eventually reach such a state of imbalance that measures need to be taken to restrict the growth of metropolitan areas. In Sweden and the Netherlands the shift in the migration policy could be clearly seen: to relieve the congestion in the concentration areas the governments decided to try and spread population and employment.

As discussed earlier, migration in countries that are still at the urbanization stage, like Hungary and Poland, has invoked similar efforts on the part of the government to direct urban development in the concentration areas.

A reverted migration policy is one way the government can restrict urban growth. It is clearly oriented towards urban development, extended now to places where there has been no such development as yet. So, a policy aimed at dispersing people and jobs away from congested areas may be explicitly urban from two points of view: from that of the concentration area and from that of the area selected for the location of people and employment.

Finally a form of migration policy may be mentioned that represents a synthesis of those already described, serving both regional stimulation and urban deconcentration. In this policy the government supports migration only as far as it is oriented towards specific places in problem areas that have been chosen as key-points for economic development, a variation commonly known as growth-pole strategy. This strategy assumes that migrants from agrarian areas as well as from towns will settle in such selected cores and that industries leaving congested areas will locate there too.

In as far as such a migration policy stimulates urban growth in problem areas it is also an explicit urban policy.

It appears that this last type of migration policy, in various versions, has been operated in several countries. Its history is closely associated with regional stimulation policy, to be discussed separately in the next section.

12.3. Regional stimulation policy

12.3.1. *Motives and execution*

In general the objective of a regional stimulation policy is the promotion of economic growth in backward regions. To this end a programme of direct and indirect stimulation of economic activity is worked out.

Employment may be boosted by investment in new local projects, or by encouraging, either directly or indirectly, the migration of existing enterprises from other regions. Efficiency demands that any kind of stimulation will be given to regions that are ripe for development or at any rate have some potential.

The impression is gained from recent European experience that in general governments do not proceed to the effective stimulation of weak regions until certain targets of economic growth at a national level have been achieved. Before an explicit regional policy was formulated in any European country, almost invariably there were already wide gaps between the economic development of the individual regions. In that sense one may say that, in the early stages at least, regional policy was of an *ad-hoc* nature.

Moreover, it appears that regional stimulation policies were by no means exclusively motivated by the needs of backward regions, but were inspired just as much by the predicament of highly developed, urbanized, congested areas.

Regional stimulation implies first and foremost industrialization of the problem areas. Two main groups of implementary measures may be distinguished. The first group comprises all those measures by which the government directly influences regional development by setting up industrial projects as well as providing the corresponding housing facilities, infrastructure, and social amenities.

In the centrally governed countries of Eastern Europe the government is eminently equipped for such direct planning, because in those countries the government is the main, in some sectors the only, agent of investment allocation. Such apparently ideal conditions for a regional stimulation policy must not blinker one to the fact that in socialist countries, too, the spatial allocation of resources is constrained by economic laws and geographic facts.

In Western European countries the government's scope for planning is largely limited to the provision of housing, public services, and social amenities. As far as employment is concerned, private enterprise is predominant in the Western European system, leaving the government with limited powers of action. As a consequence, regional stimulation policy in Western Europe proceeds according to mainly indirect planning measures, aimed at the creation of favourable and attractive conditions for the development of private commercial enterprise. Examples of such indirect measures are the granting of premiums and subsidies for investments, fiscal benefits or contributions towards wages in establishments setting up businesses in the regions concerned. In the direct sphere, infrastructural and social projects can be carried out to enhance the region's powers of attraction.

It must be noted, however, that in Eastern European countries also the government has limited power to control and influence urban processes. In Hungary, for instance, part of the money invested remains with an enterprise, and businesses can be encouraged to invest in certain areas by being given economic incentives, etc., and by being prohibited in others, although locations for these investments are not decided upon by the central government.

In Chapter 13 the relevance of the distinction between direct and indirect planning will be explained, and their development in the various countries will be discussed.

The last question to be dealt with in this chapter on urban policy is the extent to which a regional stimulation policy, which in all European countries has come to be an explicit part of economic policy since 1945, has represented an effective strategy in urban development. As an introduction to subsection 12.3.2 devoted to this subject, a few remarks are in order.

There appear to have been considerable differences in the extent to which various countries have tried to effectuate a specific pattern of urban growth in problem areas. In most cases, the idea of urban planning as an integral part of regional policy was hardly noticeable in the early stages. Nor was there a clear concept of a strategy for regional economic development, certainly not in any elaborate form. In the first instance, efforts at regional stimulation were often too scattered to be of much help; no heed was given to the demands of efficiency or to the degree of maturity of the regions involved. In Belgium, for instance, but also in other countries, regional policy was directed for quite a time to a great number of centres; controlled and scattered spatial development resulted.

Having learnt from experience, most governments in due course became convinced that a regional policy can only be successful if it is oriented towards a limited number of carefully selected cores of development. Such a regional policy was expected to be much more effective for regional economic growth. With the introduction of such an oriented development strategy, regional stimulation policy acquired a much more distinctive urban character. This aspect is the subject of subsection 12.3.2.

12.3.2. *Regional policy as a form of explicit urban planning*

A regional stimulation policy by which support is concentrated mainly on a limited number of growth centres selected for the purpose is commonly called a "growth-pole policy". It is based on the conviction that only a strategy of spatial concentration can lead to optimum economic growth.

The initial aim of the growth-pole strategy was to improve the regional income and employment situation. Promotion of urban growth was not counted among the main objectives. Obviously, however, the economic stimulation of selected development centres implies urban growth in those centres; in that sense a growth-pole strategy is, implicitly at least, an element of urban policy.

It has been observed that the growth-pole strategy, implemented within the range of a policy of regional economic stimulation, tended to be operated more and more explicitly in several countries as the initiation of an urban-growth process. Several explanations offer themselves. First, it appears that the urban problems in congestion areas have inspired policy-makers to formulate plans for urban development in underdeveloped regions. Their experience in congested towns led them to try for a more balanced distribution of urban growth. Deconcentrated urbanization to relieve congestion was combined with the stimulation of weak regions elsewhere. In France and Poland, for instance, the elaboration of plans for a national urbanization system was initiated in this way. It all began with the need to spread urban centres over a wider area, this implying the founding of new towns in areas that had so far remained rural. Regional policy had to be reoriented: from then on the stimulation policy also had to bring about the formation of the desired polycentric national system.

The government was able to bring about the migration of certain activities from the congested areas to the cores to be stimulated according to the national plan. It could do this successfully because the urban deconcentration policy was consistent with the regional stimulation policy. Even in

countries that do not suffer from acute congestion in their large towns—
Bulgaria would be a case in point—policy-makers are becoming aware that
the problems of backward regions are essentially problems of urban development. For that reason their regional policy, too, is oriented more than it
used to be towards explicit stimulation of urban growth in such areas, with
a view to establishing a national urbanization pattern.

The desire for a polycentric development was first expressed in France,
in the so-called policy of the "métropoles d'équilibre". We consider the
introduction of that concept an important step towards a national urban
policy, and shall, therefore, give special attention to its history in France.

In France the first step in the direction of a national urban hierarchy was
taken in the fifth Five Year Plan (1966–1970). In that plan, the ideas
referred to above about the formation of urban centres of gravity outside
Paris were presented as concrete policy objectives. The concept of "métropoles d'équilibre" had been derived from the growth-pole theory elaborated by Perroux. The metropolises were to be conceived of as selected
development centres which were finally to counterbalance the Paris agglomeration. This was a clear example of a dispersal policy aiming at the
same time to check the over-rapid growth of Paris and to stimulate economic progress in problem areas. Eight large centres, distributed across the
whole of France, were earmarked for development into "métropoles d'équilibre".

It was considered a prerequisite for the preservation of existing and the
attraction of new industrial enterprises that the growth poles would have a
high level of amenities, and the location of tertiary activities in the selected
towns was stimulated accordingly.

In the course of time the strategy described developed more and more
into an element of a national urbanization policy. It was found necessary
to complete the system of "métropoles" with a lower level of urban hierarchy. In the next Five Year Plan (1971–1975) special attention was given,
therefore, to the development of so-called "villes moyens", towns with a
population of between 20,000 and 200,000. Their development was required
to prevent a "desert" from being left around the metropolises, as there used
to be around Paris, on a national scale.

Since 1975 policy seems to have been oriented mainly to the lowest level
of the urban hierarchy: that of small centres.

We would summarize recent French urban policy as follows: the policy
of the "métropoles d'équilibre" may be looked upon as a strategy for
regional stimulation according to the growth-pole concept, whose primary
concern was, however, to relieve the congestion in the Paris region. French
regional policy may be considered, therefore, as derived from and complementary to the urban policy in the Paris region. That is where France

differs from Bulgaria, for instance, where the problems of the weak regions were the main reason for the establishment of a national urban policy.

We conclude that the formulation of a national urban policy has been based on consistent urban deconcentration and regional stimulation, which led more or less automatically to the integration of different spatial sub-policies, and thus to a national urban policy.

However, in the last few years developments can be observed in various countries that herald the disappearance of the correspondence between regional and urban policy. The reason is that the urban concentration areas, which up till now counted as strong areas, are increasingly becoming problem areas themselves, particularly in the inner parts of these cities. It appears that unemployment, which used to be the lot of weak, less-urbanized areas, has now become most serious in large towns, for example in Britain and the Netherlands.

Recent developments have led to another reorientation in regional and urban policy. National urban policy is being aimed at the reurbanization of existing large towns rather than at deconcentrated urbanization.

The conclusion to be drawn from the history of regional policy, considered from an urban point of view, is that three stages can be identified. First, the stage in which a policy of regional stimulation is carried on independently of other spatial sub-policies. In that stage the primary objective is mostly economic growth; according to the stimulation strategy adopted, more or less rapid urban growth will occur. Regional stimulation policy in the first stage has an implicitly urban character.

Typically, in the next stage deconcentration is aimed at relieving the congestion in large towns; the formation of national urban systems comes about. Regional stimulation policy is directed towards the promotion of urban growth in problem regions, and so becomes explicitly urban in character. Finally an evolution can be observed in which regional stimulation and the deconcentration of enterprises from congested areas are no longer automatically associated. This new evolution is caused by, among other things, the rapid rise in unemployment and social deprivation in the metropolitan areas of some countries, invoking increasing resistance to a policy that aims at restricting employment growth from such urban areas.

In the next chapter the function of urban planning in the various countries will be examined more closely.

13

The Nature of Planning[1]

In most countries urban policy has to a large extent the nature of physical planning. Physical planning could be defined as "arranging in a feasible and acceptable way" or as "devising procedures to accomplish a feasible and acceptable arrangement".

In *direct positive planning* the elements that are to be planned are directly arranged in a certain order. That is what happens when a room is being furnished: the available furniture is placed about the room in an orderly way. It is therefore an example of *direct* arranging: order is created by arranging the elements in a pattern thought desirable.

However, a similar result achieved here in a positive way, that is, when the planner himself performs all the operations needed to create the desired order, can in principle also be accomplished in a negative way.

Suppose there are three elements, A, B, and C, to be arranged in an acceptable and feasible way. The space available consists of three cells. Suppose further that the "ideal" order, that is the order that is ideal in the eyes of the government, would be A in the first cell, B in the second, and C in the third, thus:

A	B	C

The desired results could have been achieved by operating the following "position rules":

1. A, B, and C are to be placed in the three cells 1, 2, and 3;
2. B and C must not go into the first cell;
3. A and B must not go into the third cell;
4. A and C must not go into the second cell.

[1] The first part of this paragraph leans heavily on L. H. Klaassen and J. H. P. Paelinck, "Spatial planning: a tentative solution?" in *Economic Problems Galore*, Rotterdam University Press, 1975.

Such negative positioning by means of marginal conditions would result in exactly the same layout as positive arranging, though the starting-points are entirely different.

The first process, that of positive planning, comes close to the physical planning procedures followed in socialist countries; the second, negative procedure comes much closer to the planning in market economies. Positive, direct planning implies authority on the planners' part to arrange elements directly and positively according to a certain pattern; in the other approach to planning no such authority is required, but the planner must have power to prevent, say, A being placed in the second cell. In the former case the planner has direct authority to place elements where he wants them, or he is in a position to command somebody else to place them so. In the latter case, the result is achieved by prohibition, rather than by command, which implies that the responsibility for placing the elements lies with somebody else. In positive planning the full responsibility for the final outlay rests with the planning authority.

As already stated, direct positive planning is the regular procedure in socialist countries. In Western countries this kind of planning is only performed by the authorities in as far as they control some of the elements: roads, public enterprises, universities, etc. The location of industrial plants is established in a negative way by the allocation of certain sites to industry. Actually, such allocation only means that industry is not prohibited from locating itself on the site in question. The government can only control the location of government enterprises; in other cases the decision lies with companies themselves.

Two implications have been made above which need further consideration. The first is that the order ultimately achieved does not depend on whether the arrangement was done in a positive or negative way; the second is that prohibitive and/or mandatory stipulations have no bearing on what actually happens.

Imagine that the order A–B–C is the ideal one from the government's point of view, but that from a commercial point of view B must not be established in cell 2 because it would not be profitable to put it there; in that case the "ideal" arrangement will not materialize because element B will drop out of the planning procedure. In the case of a market economy such a situation would result from the decision of the entrepreneur; in a socialist economy it could result from a disagreement between the physical planning authorities and the ministry of industry. Now the question arises whether A–B–C can still be looked upon as the "best" arrangement; in other words whether it remains wise, now that industries or the ministry fail to show themselves anxious to locate a plant at the planned industrial sites, to plan residential area A and infrastructure C as was provided for under the assumption that B would be realized. If the answer is no, then the whole planning procedure is unsettled. The planning order does not materialize because the prohibitive rules or the positive rules have changed the set of elements to be arranged and, consequently, the target arrangement.

Frequently, such a sequence of events leads to a revision of stipulations, notably when, in our example, pattern A–B–C seems inferior to a new arrangement B–A–C, in which industrial sites will indeed be used as such. Evidently, the arrangement originally supposed to be the ideal one can only be so if the elements A, B, and C are viable in cells 1, 2, and 3 respectively. Business must be profitable in one sense or another, the deficit of public transport must not exceed certain limits, a school must have an acceptable number of pupils, etc. In other words, the arrangement one seeks to establish by means of prohibitive or mandatory stipulations must not violate certain boundary conditions. Should these conditions be ignored, then the ideal arrangement, not being feasible, has no practical significance.

In the example given, it was assumed that certain stipulations had to be adapted because the elements figuring in the planned arrangement failed to materialize in the place provided; a negative reason. However, there are other, positive reasons for considering certain stipulations to be impracticable. Pressure may be brought to bear upon the planning authorities both in socialist countries and market economies, which is strong enough to become a positive reason for a change in policy, e.g. the revocation of certain prohibitions.

To illustrate this, one example may serve. In road construction the motto was, until quite recently, that demand must be followed. Future traffic flows were estimated on the basis of certain assumed developments and on that basis a road network of a certain capacity was designed. As road planners used to anticipate growth when building roads, the capacity of finished road sections mostly exceeded the capacity required by the traffic at the time. That means that road-building was not only demand-following but also demand-creating. The excess capacity attracted new traffic, which in turn led to the construction of new roads at a later stage. On several occasions governments and others have expressed their view that such developments must be considered undesirable, especially for certain regions (urbanized areas). A rational enough view, or so it seems, but can it be upheld?

This depends on the degree to which traffic growth is autonomous. It was hitherto assumed that traffic will grow as a result of improved infrastructure. Without denying the truth of that assumption, one may still point out that traffic also carries an element of autonomous growth, which, even if it cannot make traffic exceed the road-network capacity, can and will cause tremendous congestion unless the road capacity is adjusted. Cool planners will not let themselves be swayed by such considerations, but will maintain that their wish is precisely that the disease will burn itself out. But whether a Cabinet Minister can afford to take such a cool view does not depend on him alone, but also on the other members of the Cabinet, the members of Parliament, the electorate, the press, the influence municipalities or regional authorities involved can exert, etc. Moreover, the consequence of *not* building roads is not very clear. All the pressures and uncertainties, and the doubts which arise, will probably in some cases lead to a deviation from the original plan. If that happens, the marginal condition is evidently no longer autonomous, but has become dependent on actual development. Thus, policy becomes an endogenous factor, and the quantity to be controlled by the marginal condition becomes an endogenous variable in the model.

Although the foregoing is just one example, it justifies the query as to whether this sort of development is of a rather specific or of a more general nature. This question is vital to the problems studied in this volume. Are implicit governmental measures determined to a large extent by the developments in urban areas, or are government policies in fact responsible for these developments? It seems from the experience of urban development in different European countries, particularly in Western European countries, that, whatever the government policy in these countries regarding development in urban areas might have been, the result is more or less the same in each country and, moreover, in as far as the governments were to be held responsible for the results, does not particularly flatter the efficiency of their policies.

It appears from the information given in the national reports that:

1. policy measures in each stage of urbanization were comparable in nature;
2. each stage of urbanization was followed by the following stage in the same order for each country;
3. the present stage in many Western European countries is characterized by efforts to restore the position of central cities in functional urban regions; in Eastern Europe it is characterized by a continued strengthening of the urban centres and the search for a proper spatial policy by which to influence the direction of the suburbanization process.

The essential question to be answered in this report is whether these common features point to an autonomy of the internal dynamics of the system or whether government measures as exogenous interventions are to

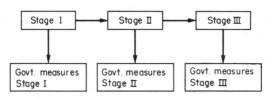

Fig. 13.1. Unsuccessful government intervention in the process of urban development.

Fig. 13.2. Successful government intervention in the process of urban development.

be held responsible for the sequence of stages. These two possibilities can be presented as in Figs. 13.1 and 13.2.

In Fig. 13.1 it is assumed that one stage of development is inevitably followed by the next stage, regardless of government intervention. In Fig. 13.2 it is assumed that conditions in one stage result in government measures that will lead to a second stage in which new measures will be taken that again result in the situation in the next stage, etc. The first situation would excuse the government from its responsibility for the present stage; the second would make it responsible for it.

It seems unlikely that both these diagrams are invalid. It would be very difficult to assume that government measures have not had any impact at all. In most cities the government, for example, actively participated in suburbanization by providing housing in suburban areas and by improving the public transport network to these areas. They made land available for offices in the central parts of the main cities and deliberately created central business districts where there used to be residential areas. The shift from the urbanization stage to the stage of suburbanization, for instance, was deliberately planned by the government in complete accord with the desire of the population. Neither of them probably realized what was actually happening. The measures are therefore to be considered successful in terms of the knowledge available at that particular stage.

It would be equally difficult to say that developments were completely autonomous. They could hardly have materialized without at least passive support from the government. The technical infrastructure needed for an effective suburbanization could only result from government action and definitely was not constructed as a result of private initiative.

It therefore seems most likely that both autonomous developments and government policy share the responsibility for the transition from one stage to another, both acting on the assumption that the next stage was to be preferred to the past stage, that the transition itself was a sign of material progress. Only in this way can the similarity in the development of so many nations be explained.

The moment has come in the present stage of reurbanization to find out if it is possible for the government to take effective measures to reverse the trend and act in contradiction to autonomous development. For the first time in urban history the two will have to deviate from each other. The trend is desurbanization; the government's objective is reurbanization. It is still too early to forecast the result.

A final and very important question is whether the developments in countries where this final stage is reached will induce governments of countries still in an earlier stage or in a stage with characteristics similar to that of an earlier stage to be prepared to learn from these experiences. In other words, will they be prepared to maintain the residential areas in the centres of the central cities, centralize office buildings in secondary, easily accessible centres outside the central core, adjust their traffic infrastructure to suit such an urban structure, etc. or not? It is to be hoped that the experience of countries with cities in the later stages of development may serve as a guideline for urban policies to be pursued in countries where the disadvantages of those stages have not yet materialized.

Mathematical Appendix

1. Government Expenditure, Potentials and Welfare

1.1. Governmental welfare policy

The concepts of the potential and the social-welfare function developed earlier can be used to obtain a better insight into the regional or urban welfare policy of the government. It is the central government's responsibility to promote welfare in the whole country by means of the instruments of regional policy at its disposal. Because the welfare of a country's population is given concrete form in smaller geographical units, the government, in its policy towards the various regions of the country, will try to make the regional welfare differences as small as possible, or at any rate to ensure to every region a certain minimum level. One of the instruments available to the government is the amount of money spent on the components of economic and socio-cultural infrastructure, in other words, the public expenditure directed towards the increase of the various potentials that are determinants of regional welfare.

The foregoing does not imply that the government should realize in all regions exactly the same combinations of components of the regional welfare function. It does mean that within the proviso made earlier the government should try to influence the level of relevant potentials in such a way that the resulting combination brings the social welfare in every region up to a certain desired standard. That statement implies that all elements of the welfare function are in principle substitutable and that different combinations can represent one and the same welfare level. The specification of function (2.3) corresponds with this implication.

---

[1] Published earlier in *Papers of the Regional Science Association*, Vol. 36, 1975, Philadel- . phia, 1976, pp. 101 ff.

155

If the government has a certain annual budget at its disposal for increasing potentials, it is confronted with a two-sided selection problem:

(a) to decide upon the spatial allocation of governmental funds to the various regions, giving priority to regions with a relatively low welfare;
(b) to decide upon the functional allocation of funds within each region to the various welfare components, giving preference to components with the highest contribution to welfare.

The regional as well as the functional allocation of public funds is determined according to the priorities of the government, embodied in its social welfare function. In this governmental selection function which relates to the welfare of all regions together, the total welfare of all regions will be weighed as well as the various welfare components within each region. Both sorts of weighing are directly related to the actual regional situation. The increase of welfare in a lagging region contributes most to national welfare, and the rise of a relatively low potential within a region has extra priority.

The selection process is complicated by different forms of interdependences between potentials and between regions. In the next section attention will be paid to the interregional interdependences and the relations between potentials and governmental expenditure will be dealt with.

1.2. Potentials and government expenditure

Government expenditure is taken here as an instrument to increase potentials. The various ways in which a potential can be increased by means of public expenditure are evident from the potential formula:

$$\Pi_i = \sum_j q_j s_j \, e^{-\delta c_{ij}} = \sum_j x_j \, e^{-\delta c_{ij}} \tag{1.1}$$

which indicates that public outlays for a certain facility can be related to

(a) the quality of the facility, the size remaining the same;
(b) the physical size of the facility at equal quality;
(c) the quality of the transport infrastructure.

Government expenditure is distinguished into current expenditure and capital expenditure or investments. In the following we shall restrict ourselves to public investments for net expansions of the physical size of facilities at equal quality. In that case the increase of a potential equals:

$$\Delta \Pi_i^v = \sum_j \Delta x_j^v \, e^{-\delta c_{ij}}. \tag{1.2}$$

Put:

$$\Delta x_j^v = k_j^v I_j^v \tag{1.3}$$

in which k_j^v represents the additional size of facility v that can be produced in region j with a unit-of-investment amount I_j; then it follows that:

$$I_j^v = \frac{1}{k_j^v} \Delta x_j^v = p_j^v \Delta x_j^v \tag{1.4}$$

in which p_j^v represents the price of a unit added to the size of facility v in region j in terms of the governmental capital outlay needed.

From equation (1.2) it also appears that the potential of region i is determined not only by public expenditure in the area but also by the corresponding public expenditure in all other (relevant) regions, since Π_i^v is the sum of all Π_{ij}^v's. Such a spill-over or interregional interdependence is essential for a potentials-approach. When, for instance, region i invests in educational facilities, not only will the educational potential in i, and thus the welfare level of i, increase, but the educational potentials and thus the welfare of all other regions will also be influenced by those investments, though only to the extent to which the educational facilities of region i are accessible to other regions.

Reversely, the welfare of i is influenced by investments in, for example, recreational facilities in another region, provided that the costs of transport from i to that region are not prohibitive. The picture would be very complicated, if attention should also be paid to a mutual dependence of potentials. For the sake of clarity we shall abstract from this sort of interdependence.

In principle the government can spend the total net amount of investments on all potentials in all regions, so that we may write for the government's budget relation:

$$\overline{Y} = \sum_j (I_j^h + I_j^v + I_j^w) \tag{1.5}$$

or:

$$\overline{Y} = \sum_j p_j^h \Delta x_j^h + \sum_j p_j^v \Delta x_j^v + \sum_j p_j^w \Delta x_j^w. \tag{1.6}$$

Simplified, it can be stated that unit investment prices in all regions are identical per facility, so that (1.6) changes into:

$$\overline{Y} = p^h \sum_j \Delta x_j^h + p^v \sum_j \Delta x_j^v + p^w \sum_j \Delta x_j^w. \tag{1.7}$$

We will investigate the problems of governmental welfare policy somewhat closer in the next section.

2. Optimum Allocation of Welfare Investments

2.1. Approach for two facilities and n regions

Assume that the welfare function for the ith region consists of two elements Π_{1i} and Π_{2i}, defined (as before) as

$$\Pi_{1i} = \sum_j x_{1j} e^{-\delta_1 c_{ij}} \tag{2.1}$$

and

$$\Pi_{2i} = \sum_j x_{2j} e^{-\delta_2 c_{ij}}. \tag{2.2}$$

The values for Π_{1i} and Π_{2i} at the beginning of the year under consideration are indicated by $\Pi_{1i}^{(0)}$ and $\Pi_{2i}^{(0)}$, respectively.

In the analysis it is assumed that the attraction element in each region j is defined by x_j, regardless of the number of people using the facility. Obviously this assumption restricts the validity of the analysis but enables us to keep the argument relatively simple. A more complete analysis could be made by assuming that the attractiveness of x_j declines (or increases) with the number of people attracted by it.

We now assume that the government divides a given sum of money among the regions and the (two) facilities in such a way that the *increase* in the welfare of all regions together is maximized. We shall assume a very simple welfare function. Write:

$$W_i = (\Pi_{1i})^{\alpha_1}(\Pi_{2i})^{\alpha_2} \tag{2.3}$$

and consequently

$$\varphi = \Delta W_i = (\Pi_{1i}^{(0)} + \Delta\Pi_{1i})^{\alpha_1}(\Pi_{2i}^{(0)} + \Delta\Pi_{2i})^{\alpha_2} - (\Pi_{1i}^{(0)})^{\alpha_1}(\Pi_{2i}^{(0)})^{\alpha_2} \tag{2.4}$$

from which it follows that

$$d\varphi_i = \alpha_1 \frac{W_i^{(1)}}{\Pi_{1i}^{(0)} + \Delta\Pi_{1i}} \, d\Delta\Pi_{1i} + \alpha_2 \frac{W_i^{(1)}}{\Pi_{2i}^{(0)} + \Delta\Pi_{2i}} \, d\Delta\Pi_{2i}. \qquad (2.5)$$

Write:

$$\Delta\Pi_{1i} = \sum_j v_{1j} \, e^{-\delta_1 c_{ij}} \quad \text{and} \quad \Delta\Pi_{2i} = \sum_j v_{2j} \, e^{-\delta_2 c_{ij}} \qquad (2.6)$$

in which

$$v_{1j} = \Delta x_{1j} \quad \text{and} \quad v_{2j} = \Delta x_{2j}. \qquad (2.7)$$

Then

$$d\varphi_i = \alpha_1 \frac{W_i^{(1)}}{\Pi_{1i}^{(0)} + \Delta\Pi_{1i}} \sum_j e^{-\delta_1 c_{ij}} \, dv_{ij} + \alpha_2 \frac{W_i^{(1)}}{\Pi_{2i}^{(0)} + \Delta\Pi_{2i}} \sum_j e^{-\delta_2 c_{ij}} \, dv_{2j} \qquad (2.8)$$

and

$$d\varphi = \sum_i d\varphi_i = \alpha_1 \sum_i \frac{W_i^{(1)}}{\Pi_{1i}^{(0)} + \Delta\Pi_{1i}} \sum_j e^{-\delta_1 c_{ij}} \, dv_{1j}$$

$$+ \alpha_2 \sum_i \frac{W_i^{(1)}}{\Pi_{2i}^{(0)} + \Delta\Pi_{2i}} \sum_j e^{-\delta_2 c_{ij}} \, dv_{2j}. \qquad (2.9)$$

An alternative approach would be to assume a "government" welfare function in which the national welfare is a function of the welfare levels of each individual region:

$$\varphi = \varphi(\varphi_1, \ldots, \varphi_n) \qquad (2.10)$$

so that

$$d\varphi = \sum_i \varphi_i' \, d\varphi_i \qquad (2.11)$$

in which the weight φ_i' would be a declining function of the welfare level of the ith region. We will continue the argument with the simple assumption that

$$d\varphi = \sum_i d\varphi_i,$$

in which all weights are equal to unity.

Now assume a budget restriction

$$\overline{Y} = p_1 \sum_j v_{1j} + p_2 \sum_j v_{2j} \qquad (2.12)$$

in which $\overline{Y}$ is the sum of money the government is willing and able to spend freely (i.e. after deduction of the running costs of the facilities already existing at the beginning of the year).

We now write

$$d\overline{Y} = 0 = p_1 \sum_j dv_{1j} + p_2 \sum_j dv_{2j} \qquad (2.13)$$

and can derive the following first-order equilibrium conditions:

$$\frac{\partial \varphi}{\partial v_{1j}} = \alpha_1 \sum_i \frac{W_i^{(1)} e^{-\delta_1 c_{ij}}}{\Pi_{1i}^{(0)} + \Delta\Pi_{1i}} = \lambda p_1 \qquad (2.14)$$

$$\frac{\partial \varphi}{\partial v_{1k}} = \alpha_1 \sum_i \frac{W_i^{(1)} e^{-\delta_1 c_{ik}}}{\Pi_{1i}^{(0)} + \Delta\Pi_{1i}} = \lambda p_1 \qquad (2.15)$$

$$\frac{\partial \varphi}{\partial v_{2j}} = \alpha_2 \sum_i \frac{W_i^{(1)} e^{-\delta_2 c_{ij}}}{\Pi_{2i}^{(0)} + \Delta\Pi_{2i}} = \lambda p_2 \qquad (2.16)$$

$$\frac{\partial \varphi}{\partial v_{2k}} = \alpha_2 \sum_i \frac{W_i^{(1)} e^{-\delta_2 c_{ik}}}{\Pi_{2i}^{(0)} + \Delta\Pi_{2i}} = \lambda p_2. \qquad (2.17)$$

The unknowns in these equations are the v_{1j}'s, the v_{2j}'s and λ, together $2n + 1$ in number. The number of equations equals $2n$ plus the budget restriction, i.e. also $2n + 1$. This means that the unknowns can in principle be determined as functions of the existing levels x_{1j} and x_{2j}, the distances c_{ij}, the two prices p_1 and p_2, and total government expenditures $\overline{Y}$.

Although the equations look rather daunting, it may be remarked that the analysis results in a two-fold optimization procedure, viz. first, finding the optimum distribution of new facilities over the regions, and second, finding the optimum expenditure on each facility. The first result may be written as

$$\frac{\partial \varphi}{\partial v_{ij}} = \frac{\partial \varphi}{\partial v_{1k}}, \quad \text{and alternatively} \quad \frac{\partial \varphi}{\partial v_{2j}} = \frac{\partial \varphi}{\partial v_{2k}}, \qquad (2.18)$$

indicating that the marginal utility of the additional facility in j should equal the marginal utility of the additional facility in k.

The second may be written as:

$$\frac{\partial \varphi / \partial v_{1j}}{\partial \varphi / \partial v_{2j}} = \frac{p_1}{p_2}, \quad \forall j. \qquad (2.19)$$

A well-known formula, indicating that the ratio of the marginal utilities of facilities 1 and 2 should equal the ratio of their prices.

2.2. The solution of the system

The first-order conditions allow for the following solution procedure. Write

$$z_{1i} = \alpha_1 \frac{W_i}{\Pi_{1i}}, \tag{2.20}$$

$$z_{2i} = \alpha_2 \frac{W_i}{\Pi_{2i}}. \tag{2.21}$$

Then the equation (2.14) may be written as

$$\sum_i z_{1i} e^{-\delta_1 c_{ij}} = \lambda p_1, \quad \forall j \tag{2.22}$$

or, in matrix notation,

$$z'_1 D_1 = i' \lambda p_1 \tag{2.23}$$

in which D_1 is the matrix of distance elements.
Similarly we write for the second facility

$$z'_2 D_2 = i' \lambda p_2. \tag{2.24}$$

From (2.23) and (2.24) we derive the values for z'_1 and z'_2

$$z'_1 = i' D_1^{-1} \lambda p_1 \tag{2.25}$$

and

$$z'_2 = i' D_2^{-1} \lambda p_2. \tag{2.26}$$

We proceed by rewriting (2.20) and (2.21) as

$$\frac{W_i}{\Pi_{1i}} = \Pi_{1i}^{\alpha_1-1} \Pi_{2i}^{\alpha_2} = \frac{z_{1i}}{\alpha_1}, \tag{2.27}$$

$$\frac{W_i}{\Pi_{2i}} = \Pi_{1i}^{\alpha_1} \Pi_{2i}^{\alpha_2-1} = \frac{z_{2i}}{\alpha_2}, \tag{2.28}$$

or as:

$$\ln \frac{z_{1i}}{\alpha_1} = (\alpha_1 - 1) \ln \Pi_{1i} + \alpha_2 \ln \Pi_{2i}, \tag{2.29}$$

$$\ln \frac{z_{2i}}{\alpha_2} = \alpha_1 \ln \Pi_{1i} + (\alpha_2 - 1) \ln \Pi_{2i}. \tag{2.30}$$

From these i sets of equations all Π_{1i} and Π_{2i} may be derived. Since the $\Pi_{1i}^{(0)}$ and $\Pi_{2i}^{(0)}$ are known, all $\Delta\Pi_{1i}$ and $\Delta\Pi_{2i}$ can be computed.
Since, furthermore,

$$v'_1 D_1 = \Delta\Pi'_1 \tag{2.31}$$

and

$$\mathbf{v}_2' D_2 = \Delta \Pi_2' \tag{2.32}$$

we find

$$\mathbf{v}_1' = \Delta \Pi_1' D_1^{-1} \tag{2.33}$$

and

$$\mathbf{v}_2' = \Delta \Pi_2' D_2^{-1}. \tag{2.34}$$

It appears that the values of the v's can be derived in a fairly straight-forward way from the first-order equilibrium conditions. It should be noted, however, that the solution of the system has one important restriction, viz. that all $v \geq 0$. This should, of course, be taken into account, by rewriting (2.14) through (2.17) as Kuhn-Tucker rather then as Lagrange conditions.[2]

[2] Credits J. H. P. Paelinck.